Unholy Water?

Ffynnon Elian, 'The Cursing Well'.

By Jane Dryhurst Beckerman.

Illustrations by Susan McKenna.

Dedication and acknowledgements.

This book is dedicated to the memory of William Dryhurst Roberts, my grandfather. Born in 1881, he grew up in Lon Cariadon in Denbigh, with 10 brothers and 2 sisters, in the butcher's shop of his father, Hugh Dryhurst Roberts, one-time Mayor of Denbigh. In 1919, married with two children, he bought a 65-acre farm called Cefn-y-Ffynnon in Llanelian, Colwyn Bay.

In Cae Ffynnon Elian (St Elian's well field) is the holy well of St Elian, Ffynnon Elian, known from the end of the 18th century as 'the Cursing Well'. My interest in the well began as I listened to Grandpa talk about it. His great, great grandchildren: Gabriel, Barbara, Freda, Hope, Acer, Charlie, Miles, Harriet, Florence, Ethan, Rosemary and Hannah, will now be able to learn more of the singular history of this corner of the farm in Wales.

Tristan Gray Hulse and Janet Bord have provided inspiration, information, unstinting help and a genuine interest in the project. They have saved me from far too many errors to catalogue; the ones that remain are all mine.

Sincere thanks to Mike Green and Gill Jones for help in unravelling the family tree of the Pughs of Penrhyn.

Contents.

Chapter One.   Ffynnon Elian before it became 'the Cursing Well'. p. 7.

Chapter Two. The years as 'the Cursing Well'. p. 15.

Chapter Three. The first court case in 1818. p. 27.

Chapter Four. The Nonconformist movement and Capel Nant Meifod. p. 32.

Chater Five. Jac Ffynnon Elian and the court case in 1831. p. 39.

Chapter Six. The last years at Ffynnon Elian. p. 44.

Chapter Seven. Stories about the well. p. 48.

***

Appendix One. Ownership of Ffynnon Elian. p.56.

Appendix Two. Saint Elian. p. 71.

Appendix Three. Holy Wells in Wales in the Reformation. p.76.

Appendix Four. Cursing ritual. p. 78.

Introduction.

The holy well of St Elian, Ffynnon Elian ('ffynnon' is the Welsh word for a well, a spring or a source), in North Wales, is one of many hundreds of holy wells throughout Britain. Holy wells are those often named for a saint, water sources that are believed to have spiritual power but Ffynnon Elian has an unusually dark and complex history. The holy well of St Elian became known throughout Britain from the end of the 18th century as 'the Cursing Well'. By the middle of the 19th century the name of 'the Cursing Well' had reached India, and readers of early 19th century magazines and newspapers enjoyed sensational reports of the malice and evil that was said to take place there. It was said that people had died as a direct result of being cursed at Ffynnon Elian, or had lived out their lives in fear and dread.

This is the history of a unique phenomenon. No other saints well has been used in such different ways over hundreds of years, or been described in such an 'unholy' fashion. The history of Ffynnon Elian reflects Welsh religious and social change from the 16th century onwards and illustrates the image of the Welsh in the eyes of their English neighbours.

Ffynnon Elian is within a mile of the North Wales coastline, about half way between the cathedral towns of Bangor and St Asaph. Within a short walking distance of the holy well is the church of St Elian in the village of Llanelian-yn-Rhos, and between the well and the church stands a small, now-disused Methodist chapel known as Capel Nant Meifod. With the old farmhouse that stands at the top of the well field called Cefn-y-Ffynnon (the ridge or the back of the well), this holy well, chapel and church, within a few hundred yards of one another, were the stage for an unfolding drama of conflicting systems of belief.

Ffynnon Elian today.

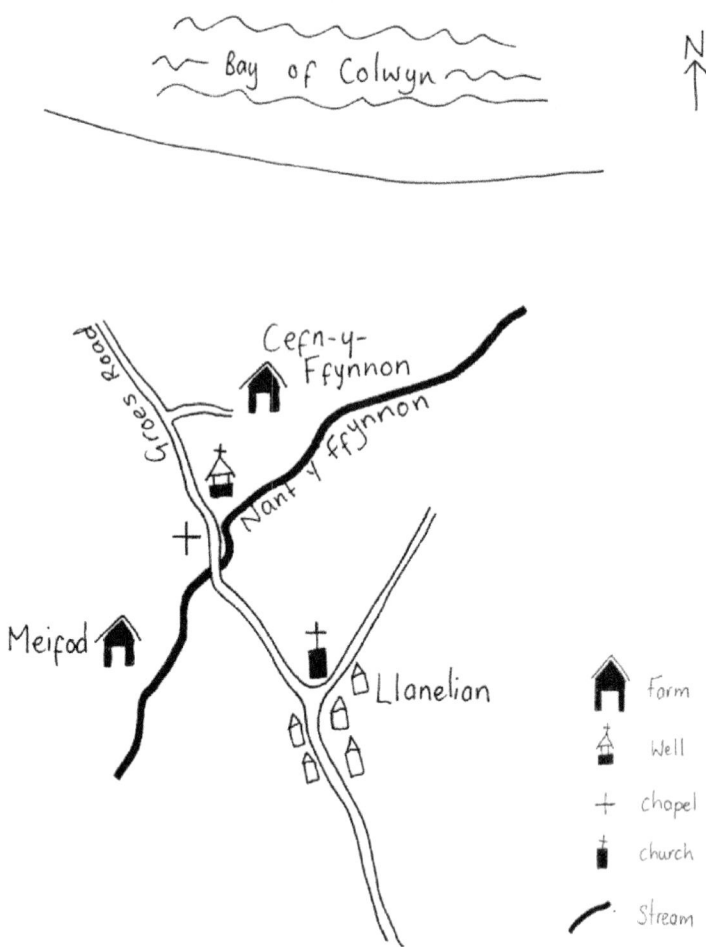

Map of church and chapel, farm, well

Ffynnon Elian, before it became 'the Cursing well'.

The earliest-known tale of the power of the well reveals the reputation of Ffynnon Elian in the early 18th century. The 'Coverlet Story' comes from a report[1] written circa 1775 for Thomas Pennant (1726-1798), naturalist, traveller, antiquarian and writer, who lived all his life at Downing Hall in Flintshire. Thomas Pennant travelled around Wales with a view to writing an account of his travels, and *A Tour in Wales* was published in three volumes in 1778, 1781 and 1783. He wasn't able to speak Welsh and took the prudent precaution of sending ahead a personal representative, who could report back to him with the more interesting or unusual events or places that Pennant might wish to include in his book. This report, now in the National Library of Wales, was almost certainly written by Rev. John Lloyd, the vicar of Caerwys and a personal friend of Pennant. It contains a lengthy section on Ffynnon Elian that includes the following story, told by a 'gentleman' who had in turn been told by 'the old woman who had then the care of the well [who] remembered a most extraordinary circumstance, which greatly raised the reputation of their saint':

> The story is thus told. A woman who lived in the parish of Llandegla; having lost a coverlet, desired a neighbour of hers to accompany her to Ffynnon Elian, in hopes of regaining her property, & discovering the offender. To this her neighbour readily assented: and away the gossips trudged, to visit good St Hilary.[2] Being arrived at the place, & having offered up their prayers at the well, they, as was usually done in similar cases, repaired to the church of Llanelian or St. Hilary. The two devotees having put some money in the poor's box which is said to be dedicated to the memory of the saint, kneeled before the altar and prayed that St. Hilary would discover to them the thief, & restore the coverlet to its owner. After the good woman who had lost the coverlet had finished her devotions, she got up and sauntered up and down the church for some time, waiting for her companion. For some while imagining her companion was offering up some private ejaculations, she did not interrupt her. But after a considerable time had elapsed, she with some surprize asked the other why she continued so long in that kneeling posture. The poor wretch who was still kneeling begged of the good woman, whom she had presumptuously attended on this solemn

---

[1] National Library of Wales MS 2594E.

[2] The names of St Hilary and St Elian are used interchangeably in many documents. See appendix 'St. Elian'.

occasion, that she would forgive her the injury she had done her. She then immediately confessed that she was the thief who had stolen the coverlet, that she found herself from some supernatural cause, as she supposed, utterly unable to move from the spot she then kneeled upon, and that she was convinced she must continue in that same posture until she should be freely forgiven by the person whom she had so grossly injured. The offended party instantly and generously forgave the poor penitent, who in consequence thereof, immediately recovered the use of her limbs, & was glad to get home again; fully resolved never more to dare or provoke the great St. Hilary. This story, extravagant as it may seem, is still related & firmly believed by many, who, in other respects, are deemed persons of sense and understanding.

As a story designed to confirm the perceived powers of Ffynnon Elian and the spread of its influence, this was obviously a memorable success. The writer of the report, while carefully distancing 'persons of sense and understanding' from superstitious belief, tells the story respectfully and without irony. Immediately noteworthy is that Llandegla is 36 miles away from Ffynnon Elian. The women could have visited St Winefride's well, the most famous holy well in Wales. Llandegla itself had a healing, holy well (named after St. Tegla). They passed several other holy wells on their way to Ffynnon Elian. We do not know what other means of recovery the 'good woman' may have tried and a coverlet does not sound important enough to warrant such a lengthy journey with its expense, trouble and the delegating of normal responsibilities.

With this story, however, the reputation of Ffynnon Elian as a site of 'natural justice' was established. The report written for Pennant in 1775 provides a detailed snapshot of the well-house itself with an attached bathing place where the visitor could immerse him- or her-self in the waters of the holy well:

> [the well is] within a square inclosure, walled round, four yards each way. Into this inclosure we get over a stone stile. In the middle of it stands the fountain likewise walled round, except on the south side where is a wicket locked. The inner wall surrounding the fountain is also square, about a yard high, & of the same dimension from one corner to the other. It is sodded over, & upon each corner is placed a loose stone of an uncommon form, almost in the shape of a bowl. These stones are still held sacred by the ignorant country people, & are called Bara Elian or St Hilary's bread. Within half a yard of the fountain,

on the north west angle is another spring, about a foot square. About sixty yards south of Fynnon Elian is a bath or bathing place in the property of John Holland of Teyrdan Esq, erected about ten years ago at the expence of the parish of Llanelian. It is walled round, is constantly supplied with water from the well, is a little more than two yards high, about six long & four broad, & is well flagged. It has a floodgate at the lower end of it, to let out the water, when it wants to be cleaned. We descend into the bath by a flight of eight or nine steps. All this was done for the convenience and encouragement of those devotees who come & offer up their vows to the tutelar saint of the place.

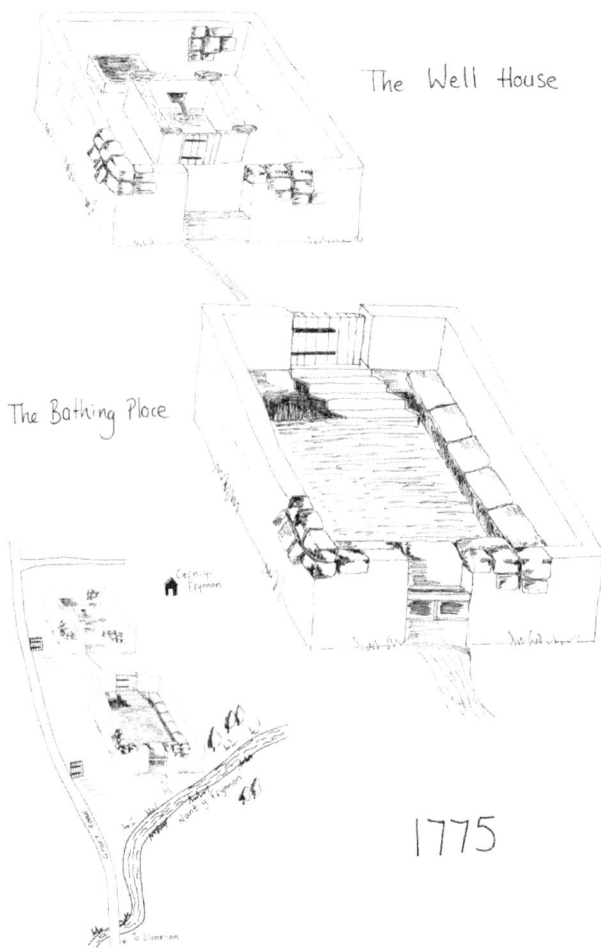

Artist's impression of the well and bathing pool from 1775 report.

The report also gives an indication of the longevity of use at Ffynnon Elian, stating, 'But the well now & for more than two hundred years past [was] much resorted to & distinguished by the name of Ffynnon Elian…'. Rev. John Lloyd then clearly outlines the reasons for coming to St Elian's well:

> This well has been formerly much resorted to, & is still in some degree by those who labour under any infirmity of mind or body; who after invoking the saint of the place if they happen to recover, attribute it intirely to his gracious interposition.
>
> Others repair hither to curse their neighbours or others who may have disobliged them, & to pray that sudden death or some dreadful calamity may not fail to overtake them. By offering up their devotions at the well & depositing some money in the poor's box in Llanelian church, they make no doubt of obtaining their requests, be they ever so unreasonable.
>
> Others again who had been robbed of their property have repaired hither & prayed to St Hilary that he would discover to them the thief, & enable them to recover what had been stolen from them.

The complexity of function at Ffynnon Elian in 1775 and the range of powers it was believed to have had are clearly outlined here. The well was visited in the hope of a cure for mental or physical illness, to curse, and for the return of lost property. The reason for the two women coming from Llandegla now becomes clearer. Petitioners came to Ffynnon Elian to ask for healing, to right the wrongs that they felt had been done to them, to seek redress, or to seek vengeance. This is not the traditional image of pilgrimage or devotion at holy wells, an image usually concerned with seeking physical or spiritual healing, absolution and closer union with God.

These years at the end of the 18th century represent a high point in the life of Ffynnon Elian. The 1775 report describes a holy well that was valued by both church and local community and that had an established reputation for the recovery of lost or stolen goods. At the same time Ffynnon Elian was also somewhere that could be used to curse, to seek vengeance for perceived wrongs. This darker, potentially dangerous reputation is not illustrated in the report, nor is it especially highlighted or commented on. It is listed as the second of the three functions of Ffynnon Elian, and the tone of the writer does not vary when reporting it. Financial benefits to the church are mentioned in connection with cursing. It seems that the complex functions at Ffynnon Elian were acceptable to both church and community.

The bathing pool described in the 1775 report was not on Cefn-y-Ffynnon land but on land owned by John Holland, a wealthy farmer living at adjoining Teyrdan farm. The pool was added to the well structure in 1765 and the church helped with its construction. In the Vestry Book of Llanelian church an entry for 1765 notes that Moses Williams charged one shilling to carry building blocks for the pool to be built. The Vestry Book also records that the church paid for and placed an advertisement in the *Chester Courant* in 1765 (a newspaper that covered much of North Wales), encouraging people to come to Ffynnon Elian. Presumably the church invested financially in the well with every hope that the visitors to Ffynnon Elian would then walk the few hundred yards up the hill to the church to ask for St Elian's blessing and to put money into the *cyff* (chest). The women from Llandegla had done this fifty or more years earlier. Their long journey argues a flourishing, settled and certainly well-known destination by the beginning of the 18th century.

Ffynnon Elian was a local landmark, supported and promoted by church and community. This indisputable evidence of co-operation with an eye to financial gain between a Protestant church and a holy well of any kind, let alone one which was said to have a power as potentially troubling as cursing, has not been noted elsewhere. The bathing place is not mentioned again in later documents, but the connection between the church and the well continued.

Although there is no earlier physical description of Ffynnon Elian than that of 1775, there is one earlier written record. Edward Lhwyd (1660-1709), botanist, linguist, antiquarian, philosopher and Oxford scholar, sent out 4,000 'Parochial Queries', three to each parish, in the late 17th century, as part of his enquiry into the geography and customs of Wales. The questions took into account Lhwyd's interest in many aspects of local life in Wales, but one question specifically asked about water sources. Lhwyd travelled throughout Wales, reaching North Wales in 1699, and began publishing the responses to his questions in 1707 in *Glossography*, the first volume of a proposed much longer work. He died soon after this. In 1909 and for the succeeding two years, Rupert H. Morris edited the responses to these parish questionnaires and they were published as three supplements to *Archaeologia Cambrensis*. They have since been known as *Parochialia*. Morris judged that all the contents of *Parochialia* part 1 (1909) were Lhwyd's notes, and this is the section that includes the entry on Ffynnon Elian:

> Mae Ffynnon Elian ymhlwy Llan Drilho a Phapistiad a hen bobl ereilh a offrymma yno rottie [groats] gynt, ag etto nailh ai grottie ai gwerth o Vara. Adhuc. Arverynt dhwedyd mae'n rhaid y chwi dhyspydhy'r Ffynnon dair gwaith dros vy mhlentyn mae yn glav: a chwedi hynny offrwm Grot.
>
> Ffynnon Elian is in the Parish of Llandrillo…and Papists and other old people offer groats or bread to the value of groats. They are used to say you must throw out all the water out of the well 3 times for my sick child, then offer ye groat. [This English translation is one of many and is not likely to have been written by Lhwyd].

There is no mention here of the specific power to restore stolen property and identify the thief that drew the women of Llandegla to Ffynnon Elian a relatively short time afterwards. Nor of cursing one's neighbours. Here, Ffynnon Elian is being visited by Catholics for unexplained reasons and is also used to cure sick children. Bread or money was offered, presumably at the well as a deposition. There is no mention in *Parochialia* of a guardian at the well, although a 'woman who had care of the well' is mentioned in the 1775 report as part of the 'coverlet' story.

It is worth noting, in view of later transactions that all included money, that a groat was worth 4d at the end of the 17th century, a not inconsiderable sum. The two women in the 'coverlet' story put money in the 'poors box' in church.

A connection between these two early documents is that of the stones, *Bara Elian* (St Elian's bread), positioned on each corner of the well housing in the circa 1775 report, and the offerings of bread given by the 'papists' and 'old people' described in *Parochialia*. The gospel of Matthew 7:9 asks, 'Or what man is there of you, whom if his son ask for bread, will give him a stone?' The offering of bread at a holy well, a reminder of the Eucharistic feast and communion with God is also a reminder of this text and of the hope that accompanied visits to the well, hope that the 'bread' of life, in the form of wishes granted by St Elian could transform the 'stones' of life's problems and difficulties. Tristan Gray Hulse, in a recent unpublished article[3] finds no mention of bread used as offering in the recorded history of other holy wells, and asserts that the *Bara Elian* stones at the well house and the record of bread

---

[3] T.G. Hulse, 'Evidence for shrines and pilgrimages in Wales in the *Valor Ecclesiaticus* (1535), and is implications for the early history of Ffynnon Elian, Llandrillo-yn-Rhos.' 2017.

offerings in *Parochialia* is most unlikely to be a coincidence. He suggests the possibility of a 'miracle' of transformation associated with St Elian in the formative years of the saint's *cultus*.

Other wells are mentioned in *Parochialia*, but none is reported as being used by 'papists'. In the second half of the 16th century, after the Reformation, increasingly severe anti-Catholic measures were implemented all over Britain and certainly in North Wales. Anti-Catholic feeling had not disappeared by the end of the 17th century and the last anti-Catholic Act passed in 1610, The Oaths Act, compelled holders of certain offices, including religious ones, to actively suppress Catholic devotional behaviour and to punish non-acceptance of Protestant worship. Nationally, the last fine for recusancy was collected in 1694. In 1641 there were 34 recusants living in Denbighshire. Without written evidence of medieval pilgrimage to the well the mention of 'papists' still visiting Ffynnon Elian in the late 17th century is intriguing.

The Pughs of Penrhyn, a local Catholic, recusant family, owned Cefn-y-Ffynnon farmhouse and land that included Ffynnon Elian in 1661 and probably for years before that. In 1770 they sold Cefn-y-Ffynnon to the Rev. John Royle of Gwydir near Llanwrst, a busy market town 12 miles away from Llanelian. The possibility of the Pughs' early ownership, promotion and protection of Ffynnon Elian during the 16th and 17th centuries is explored in appendix 1.

Despite the lack of written evidence there are several indications of the existence of Ffynnon Elian before the Reformation. The holy well itself with its early Medieval design is one such, and the change of name of the nearest village, from Bodlennin to Llanelian-yn-Rhos at the beginning of the 14th century is another. A sizeable income was registered for Llanelian-yn-Rhos church in the *Valor Ecclesiasticus* of 1535, a record of the value of church property demanded by Henry Vlll as he set about changing the religious face of Britain forever. Gray Hulse considers that:

> …one can at least be reasonably certain that some form of devotional cult was generating a fairly generous annual rate of offerings in 1535 (even allowing for the subtraction of a suitable sum to the value of the minor tithes, the oblations must have been somewhere in the region of a quarter of the annual sum noted for St Winefride's Well, £10.00, which was the largest sum recorded for any Welsh shrine), most plausibly directed in some manner towards St Elian.[4]

Gray Hulse goes on to suggest that the money given at the church in both the *Parochialia* and the 1775 report, could be 'residual elements of pilgrimage visits to a cult image of the saint in his church, even though by then the [saint's] image was long gone'.[5]

An indication of the existence of Ffynnon Elian in pre-Reformation Wales is suggested by parish boundaries, established in Wales at the end of the 13th century. Ffynnon Elian and Llanelian church were separated administratively by the parish boundary between Llandrillo-yn-Rhos and Llanelian-yn-Rhos and Ffynnon Elian in the late 13th century became part of the parish of Llandrillo-yn-Rhos. This parochial separation of the holy well of St. Elian and Llanelian church, named after the same saint and sharing in his *cultus* in North Wales, suggests strongly that they were in existence before the parish boundary that separated them was drawn up.

Older commote boundaries, drawn up before parish boundaries and long before county boundaries, formed Medieval administrative units in Denbighshire. Ffynnon Elian was on the boundary between the commotes of Isdulas and Uwch Dulas, and as boundaries were drawn up with reference to known landmarks, Ffynnon Elian could have been in existence in the early Middle Ages.

Another indication of the longevity of use at Ffynnon Elian is that at the beginning of the 14th century the nearby village changed its name to Llanelian-yn-Rhos. The church always had St Elian's name but the township around it was known as Bodlenin/Bodwelenyn/Bodlennin. It is not unreasonable to suggest that by that time Ffynnon Elian and Llanelian church were becoming, or had become, important enough to warrant a linguistic signpost.

What is certain is that by 1775 Ffynnon Elian was an established holy well with a bathing pool connected to it and that very soon afterwards it became known nationally and internationally, as 'the Cursing Well'.

---

[4] 'Evidence for shrines and pilgrimages in Wales', 2017.

[5] Ibid. p.20.

The Years as the 'Cursing Well'

By the end of the 18th century the fortunes of Ffynnon Elian had begun to change. Until 1770, the estate known as 'Cefn in Eirias', or Cefn-y-Ffynnon, containing the holy well, farmhouse and land, had been owned by the Pugh family of Penrhyn, once wealthy and important landowners. They were dedicated and faithful Catholics and recusants but by the end of the 18th century their fortunes had disappeared and they no longer owned even their ancestral property of Penrhyn. They sold the Cefn-y-Ffynnon estate including Ffynnon Elian to the Royle family, from Llanwrst.

How did Ffynnon Elian, a saint's well for hundreds of years, became 'the Cursing Well' with a reputation for malice and evil that spread far into Wales and England? There were many contributing factors. The end of the 18th century saw the rise of travel and tourism in Wales. Thomas Pennant published his first volume of *A Tour in Wales* in 1778 and English travel writers began to venture into North Wales, writing for the developing English newspaper and magazine market. Thomas Pennant was the first published writer in English to describe Ffynnon Elian to a wider, changed world of industrialisation, a growing national network of communications and a sharper awareness of national 'image'. The image of Wales in much of the London press was of a superstitious, primitive and foreign country and the published articles about Ffynnon Elian that followed on from Pennant demonstrated this. Gone was the even-handed description provided by Pennant's reporter a few years before and this, by Pennant himself:

> The well of St Aelian... has been in great repute for the cures of all diseases, by means of the intercession of the saint who was first invoked by earnest prayers in the neighboring church. He was also applied to on less worthy occasions, and made the instrument of discovering thieves, and of recovering stolen goods. Some repair to him to imprecate their neighbors and to request the saint to afflict with sudden death, or with some great misfortune, any persons who may have offended them. The belief in this is still strong; for three years have not elapsed since I was threatened by a fellow (who imagined I had injured him) with the vengeance of St Aelian, and a journey to the well to curse me with effect.

Pennant probably did not visit Ffynnon Elian and it seems that his first sentences are re-written comments from the 1775 report. He acknowledges the complexity and continuity of use at Ffynnon Elian but the last sentence, containing the personal testimony of an *eminence* like Pennant having been threatened in such a manner leaves his reader surprised and interested. Although we do not learn here who could have behaved towards such an important man in this way, a later work by magistrate and land-owner Pennant sheds further light on the subject. A few years after *A Tour in Wales*, in *The History of the Parishes of Holywell and Whiteford* (1796), he writes:

> ...the farmer is obliged to give up cultivation, by reason of the depredations the poor make on the crops. They will steal the turneps before his face, laugh at him when he fumes at them and ask him how can he be in such rage over a few turneps? As a magistrate, I never had a complaint made against a turnep-stealer... incredible as it may appear, numbers of them are in fear of being cursed at St Aelian's well and suffer the due penalty of their superstition.

Pennant may be exaggerating the effects of the power of Ffynnon Elian here, although this passage paints an interesting picture of social upheaval. Could it be that Pennant, a substantial land-owner himself, had been robbed and this was why he had been 'threatened'? He knew of other farmers and land-owners who were not prepared to take the risk of being 'put in the well', or 'cursed' by someone who had taken a few 'turneps'.

Stealing 'turneps' was a response to extreme poverty and life for the poor in North Wales in the last years of the 18th century and the first few decades of the 19th was harsh. The Napoleonic Wars took men from their lives in rural Wales to fight, leaving women and children to fend for themselves. Enclosure Acts, eagerly enforced by local land-owners, rapidly took common land away from people who owned no land themselves but could graze a sheep or a cow or some geese 'on the common'. The weather was unremittingly bad for decades and the price of corn rose beyond what was affordable. Bread riots broke out all over Wales, reaching North Wales in the early years of the 19th century. Many families tried growing potatoes rather than the usual staples of barley and oats, and faced starvation when blight or bad weather ruined their crops. It is hard to feel much sympathy for Pennant's farming friends and their 'turneps', grown for cattle fodder and stolen for human food.

Pennant's personal testimony indicates that by the end of the 18th century Ffynnon Elian had acquired another function, one that strengthened belief in the power of the holy well to provide 'natural justice' for people who had no access to law and no other agency to appeal to. It seems that Ffynnon Elian's reputation for cursing was being used by the poor to avoid prosecution. It is from these last years of the 18th century, when life was increasingly difficult for people in North Wales, that Ffynnon Elian, among its other continuing uses, began to be described as somewhere that could protect the poor against the wealthy. Ffynnon Elian had been used over time for healing, to put a curse on a neighbour or to discover the identity of a thief. Now it became known as 'the Cursing Well'.

It may have been partly this socially subversive use of Ffynnon Elian that aroused such strong feelings in visiting writers about the well. Many writers copied Pennant's comments and embellished them with their own imaginations. An early and typical example from the many references to Ffynnon Elian that appeared in print from the beginning of the 19th century is from the Rev. William Bingley, who in 1804 reported in *North Wales Delineated from Two Excursions*, a 'strange custom [that] prevails in some obscure parts of North Wales which the Clergy have now almost abolished.' Bingley described the cursing ritual as taking place in 'some church dedicated to a celebrated saint', where money is offered and 'the most virulent and dreadful imprecations,' were spoken, 'calling down curses and misfortunes on the offender for generations to come.' Bingley then noted that this ceremony sometimes took place at 'some sacred well', and finished by quoting Pennant's experience of being 'cursed'.

In 1810 a reference to Ffynnon Elian appeared in a most unexpected place, a posthumously published work on the nature of Catholic Episcopy.[6] Thomas Pennant's experiences are detailed at the beginning of a seemingly unrelated appendix concerning Ffynnon Elian. Entitled 'Well-Worshipping', after quoting Pennant the author Charles O'Conor reported that 'an athletic labourer had suddenly lost all his energy of mind and all the muscular strength of a vigorous body from having been *cursed at a well*, where his name was said to be in the *book of the well*.' O'Conor continues:

> *Extract of a letter from* Tyrdan, *on the Borders of Caernarfonshire and Denbighshire, Aug.*10, 1810.

---

[6] C. O'Conor, *Columbanus ad Hermanos, or a Letter from Columbus to his Friend in Ireland, on the present mode of appointing Catholic Bishops in his Native Country.* London, 1810.

> "S. Aelian's Well is a little, dirty hole near *Tyrdan* with a broken wall around it. The *Priestess* died last year, and *left her powers* to (I think) a Captain Thomas, possibly of Downing. The manner of cursing I do not exactly know but...the name of the devoted person was written down, and put *into the well*. While they were in it, the persons were never to prosper in any undertaking, but to pine away; and die; which they generally did from the horror it impressed upon their minds...For half a crown any enemy of your's could prevail on the old woman to *put you in the well*...Nothing, I am told can be more melancholy than the appearance of people who believed themselves under this curse.. my Maid says she knows a girl who was *in the well* when she was an infant; she had fits, and used to bite and tear everybody. Her parents suspected a person who was their enemy of putting their child in, and on going to look they found she was in, and *paid a fee for getting her out*; since which time she has been well.
>
> P. S. I remember… about five or six years ago… a very principal farmer, who was prevented from prosecuting a servant who had robbed him, by the *threat of the curse of St Aelian*."

O'Conor, who is described in *The Catholic Encyclopaedia* as 'the only Irishman with whom Samual [sic] Johnson corresponded with reference to Irish literature', completed this section of his work with a paragraph congratulating a Christian bishop for daring to 'vindicate the purity of his faith, against the vilest practices of *Druidic superstition!*'

In the letter above, the well and its surroundings are vividly described as uninvitingly as possible: 'a little, dirty hole...with a broken wall around it,'. This is a visual corollary to the practices described in the letter from Teyrdan, home of the Holland family, the same family who had given permission for a bathing pool to be built on their land, connected to Ffynnon Elian, 45 years earlier. This is a dramatically different description to the portrait of Ffynnon Elian in Pennant's report but the postscript contains another example of the well being used to prevent prosecution.

However, the letter from Teyrdan did not spring from the principled objections of those concerned to suppress 'superstitious practices' in favour of modernity. The Hollands, wealthy and socially ambitious, must have been absolutely mortified to find that they were connected, through their immediate family, with Ffynnon Elian.

In 1810 the inhabitants of Teyrdan were John Holland, a 'very principal farmer', and his wife Margaret. John had inherited Teyrdan as the oldest child of his father (also John), and John and Margaret's two daughters had recently made very advantageous marriages indeed. In 1805 Mary, the elder daughter, had married into the Wynne family of Coed Coch, one of the other wealthy and important families in the vicinity of Llanelian. In the same year the younger daughter, Margaret, had married into the Yorkes of Erddig, a grander family still. The Hollands of Teyrdan were now connected by marriage with the cream of high society in North Wales. What is not found in the letter (almost certainly written by John Holland) to Charles O'Conor is the very close relationship indeed between the 'old woman', the 'priestess' at the well mentioned in the letter, and John Holland, owner of Teyrdan, himself.

In 1770, the Pugh family sold the land and buildings of the Cefn-y-Ffynnon estate to the Rev. John Royle, of Gwydir, a manor house in Llanwrst. Margaret, the oldest child of Rev. Royle and Elizabeth Myddleton his wife, was baptised in 1754 at Gwydir, and in August 1777 Margaret married the Rev. Jeoffrey Holland, by licence, in Llanrwst. Jeoffrey, baptised in 1756, was the son of John Holland (the elder) of Teyrdan, and the youngest brother of John, probable correspondent of Charles O'Conor and owner of Teyrdan in 1810. Jeoffrey Holland is documented as being the rector of Dolbenmaen[7] parish from the end of the 18th century, and Margaret, by now obviously his estranged wife, had gone back to live in her father's property, Cefn-y-Ffynnon farm, where she had become known as 'M. H-,' the 'priestess' of the well and named in one of the surviving tales of Ffynnon Elian.

That this may not have been a union that delighted the Hollands in the first place is indicated by Margaret and Jeoffrey marrying 'by licence'. Weddings were carried out by licence for several reasons. The Hardwicke Marriage Act of 1753 had regularised marriage ceremonies, promoted 'legitimacy' and was the beginning of a different attitude in Wales towards babies born of a more irregular union. A marriage conducted by licence suggests a disinclination to celebrate that looks suspiciously like serious disapprobation in a family as well-connected as the Hollands. To try to preclude gossip, and to conceal a union that was not to the families' liking, weddings were conducted by licence without banns being read out in church. Where there was a discrepancy between the social class of the bride and groom a wedding by licence

---

[7] Dolbenmaen is in the southern end of the Lleyn peninsula.

was one way to try to avoid social embarrassment. A man and a woman might themselves have chosen to marry by licence for many reasons, including opposition to their union from one or both of their families. Witnesses at the wedding of Margaret and Jeoffrey were both from her family and notably absent were the Hollands. Their son was born in 1778, suggesting that premature pregnancy was not the reason for their marriage being unwitnessed by the groom's family. Without any way of knowing the circumstances, a wedding by licence and the eventual separation of Margaret and Jeoffrey (a most unusual occurrence within a clerical family) indicate that the marriage got off to a shaky start and was not successful.

By 1810 (the year of Margaret Holland's death) the existence in a neighbouring farm of an estranged sister-in-law who had become known as the 'priestess' of a holy well could not have been welcome. Even more embarrassingly for the family, Ffynnon Elian was rapidly becoming sensationally described as 'the Cursing Well' and the Hollands, recently connected with the Yorkes and the Wynnes, two of the wealthiest dynasties in North Wales, would have been mortified. In 1765 the Hollands had agreed that a bathing place could be built attached to Ffynnon Elian. They could not have escaped the growing notoriety of 'the Cursing Well' however much they may have tried to. John Holland's letter to Charles O'Conor, whatever he might have hoped its effects would be, did nothing to stem the tide of visitors who came to Ffynnon Elian or the published accounts of what was to be found there.

In 1812, *The Beauties of England and Wales, or Delineations Topographical* by the Rev. J. Evans was published and copied Bingley's work on the well of St Elian almost word for word. After completing his paragraph on Ffynnon Elian by quoting Pennant, Rev. Evans concludes by characterising the well-users as:

> the most illiterate or vitiated parts of the community, who from the tyrannical nature of pseudo religious influence, have been kept under the worst of all slaveries, that of mental subjection.

A tone of moral outrage when writing about the well and its users began at this time with the work of Charles O'Conor, the Rev. John Evans and the Rev. William Bingley. Over the next twenty or thirty years, articles written for English magazines concluded that the transactions at the well were without exception harmful in nature, and only possible of execution because of the degraded nature of the inhabitants of North Wales. The reputation of Ffynnon Elian, once respected and upheld by the local church and community and promoted as a repository of wisdom, healing and natural justice, had now changed completely.

Edmund Hyde Hall, who paid 'detailed visits,' to Caernarfonshire from the last years of the 18th century, was the author of *A Description of Caernarvonshire 1809-1811*, published soon after the later date in the title. He was not a Welsh speaker but like Pennant, 'interpreters and guides I was never without…who seize[d] my object, enter[ed] into the spirit of my enquiries, and bec[a]me faithful conveyers of the numerous cross-questions which I have been required to repeat within every parish.' Hyde Hall commented on the active reputation for ill-wishing at Ffynnon Elian and lectured on the need for enlightenment in such a backward community, echoing a popular view of 18th and 19th century Wales:

> …in the neighbouring parish of Llanelian is [a well] which at the commencement of the nineteeth century may well be denominated a curiosity. The dread which its magical nature inspires is actually in a state of mischievous operation, not only as it is an object of terror to the ignorant, but as it serves to cultivate the very worst parts of our nature, malice and revenge. Instigated by resentment at injuries, real or supposed, the offended person repairs to the well, fees the presiding sorceress, and requires as a requital for his bounty that she will PUT INTO THE WELL the object of this wrath…hearing of the incantation performed, he [the acccursed] flies to the place of punishment, and by the payment of a counter fee procures his enlargement from this enchanted bath. "Hae nugae series ducunt in mala". [Such a series of trifles leads to a bad end.] So at least the magistrates have thought who have more than once apprehended the presiding priestess. But the knavery and the folly still continue and will continue until Education has spread herself over the land, with Knowledge and Reason in her train.

Margaret Holland is still the 'presiding sorceress' here, dating Hyde Hall's visit to before 1810. Edmund Hyde Hall is one of the commentators who wanted to assure his readers that 'the authorities' had the matter under control and that the perpetrators of what he called 'knavery and folly' were being apprehended and punished. However, Caernarfonshire Quarter Sessions Records up to 1805 do not contain any reference to Margaret Holland, or to Ffynnon Elian. Edmund Hyde Hall was possibly referring to a case in the Great Session for the County of Flint reported in the *Chester Chronicle* in 1818:

> About twelve years ago, a poor TAILOR in Flintshire was charged with stealing a goose from an old woman: she was asked how she came to suspect the offender; when she observed, that having threatened to throw his name into the 'well,' he confessed the crime!

In 1816, Edward Pugh's tour through North Wales, described in *Cambria Depicta*, was published posthumously. He had died in 1813, at the age of 52, and the work had taken him nine years to complete, making his comments contemporaneous with Hyde Hall, Rev. J. Evans and just later than Bingley and Pennant. Pugh's attitude towards the well is rather more sophisticated than that of his peers. His tone is mocking rather than condemnatory, imaginatively describing a most unlikely 'mastiff' on guard, and his interest in the outward appearance of the well marks a change in recorded responses to Ffynnon Elian. In *Cambria Depicta*, Pugh supplied a graphic verbal portrait of the well but was 'mortified' at the lack of anything exciting going on:

> I shortly came to the village of Llanelian, a few hundred yards beyond which is the famous immolating well of the same name: I saw the door open, and close by a very large mastiff dog, looking more fiercely and terrible than a whiskered soldier on guard. I approached with some caution in full hopes of coming in upon the parties in the midst of their imprecations – Caesar was civil. Listening a moment at the door, I was mortified to find no one there. The well is circular, its diameter about two feet six inches, covered with a stone arch and sods; it is enclosed by a strong, square wall, seven feet high, and situated in a close, by the road-side.

This description of the well is not of the 'little, dirty hole' as supplied by John Holland in the letter to Charles O'Conor in 1810. Pugh does not mention the bathing pool, which may of course have been dismantled by the disgruntled Hollands, but the description of the well-housing itself is similar to that of the report of 1775. Rather than fear of potential harm, Pugh registered disappointment that there was nothing much for him to see. He reported that the cursing practice at St. Elian's well was recorded in 'a book kept by the lady whose property the well is, and who has, upon this occasion, assumed the functions of officiating clergyman of the parish.' (This dates his visit to before 1810). He then commented on the legal and financial aspects of the practices at the well:

> This subject has been frequently canvassed at the quarter sessions of the county. I am informed that the late, laudable efforts of Sir Watkin Williams Wynn…have proved abortive, the well being private property. The lady who keeps it is supposed to have made, annually a pretty round sum, but it is certainly on the decline.

Edward Pugh is the first writer to emphasise the financial gain associated with Ffynnon Elian.

The Sir Watkin Williams Wynn in question was the fifth Baronet (1772 – 1840), MP for Beaumaris, 1794 – 1796, and for Denbighshire, 1796 – 1840. Despite Pugh's statement that the well had been 'frequently canvassed' at the Quarter Sessions 'of the county', as Hyde Hall had also stated, this is not supported by Flint, Denbighshire or Caernarfonshire Quarter Sessions Records. The National Library of Wales 'Crime and Punishment' website, relating to the Great Sessions records for the period, lists five crimes in connection with Llanelian-yn-Rhos between 1730 and 1830, and with the exception of the court case in 1818, there is no mention of Ffynnon Elian being involved in any of them. The well was on private property, as Pugh noted, which may explain the lack of evidence for the 'court cases' that so many writers insisted had taken place. Another possible reason for the lack of court cases may have been that the people who had been, or who thought themselves to have been, 'cursed' were not people who could afford or had access to, legal redress. It is also possible that a visit to the well was usually experienced as good value for money, securing a chance for equitable justice for wrongdoing as well as providing an opportunity to inflict malevolent harm. The fact is that there were only two known court cases in connection with the well, brought in 1818 and 1831.

If he had lived another year or two Edward Pugh could have read 'St Aelian's Well', a poem in 5 cantos self-published in London in 1814, that appeared in the same year in *The London Magazine*. In her introduction the author Charlotte Wardle announced that 'A lightsome tale is mine to tell/ The legend of a mystic well.' However, there is little that can be described as 'lightsome' in the text, in which 'Cadwallon', heir to 'Sir Gryffydd', is in love with Elen, daughter of Modred, evil knight.[8] Modred comes to St Aelian's well to curse Gryffydd, who has offended his honour, and beaten him in a horse race. 'May Gryffydd and his house sustain/ Each ill that mark'd the

---

[8] Modred is a notorious character in the Arthurian legends. He fought King Arthur at the Battle of Camlann and though bested by Arthur, he inflicted fatal wounds on the king.

outlaw'd Cain/ Until his courser yield his breath/ And in my service meet his death:'. Modred visits the '...evil hag with shrivelled hands/ full rudely marked with hideous veins/ a wooden bowl one hand retains'. In return, the 'hag' at St Aelian's well curses 'Sir Gryffydd':

> ... With muttered spell,
>
> The witch drew water from the well, -
>
> Invok'd the saint and forthwith sped
>
> Beneath the wave the mystic lead,
>
> On which Sir Gryffydd's name was read;
>
> The charm has passed her quivering lips,
>
> And now once more the bowl she dips;
>
> Beneath the darkling surface – then
>
> Repeat's her orgies o'er again;
>
> "Tis done!" she cried – a hideous yell,
>
> From lips as hideous piercing fell;
>
> Art thou of earth or fiend of hell
>
> Accursing hag of Aelian's well?

The well itself is described in similarly extravagant language: '...birds of omen harbour'd there/ And fill'd with boding shrieks the air/ The blasted trees so rent and riven/ Had proved the bolt and wrath of heaven/And deep, and dark, and dank and drear/ The baneful fountain rises here.'

The poem in its considerable entirety displayed accurate knowledge of the area surrounding the well; mountains, valleys and specific towns were named accurately. Cadwallon (sometimes Caswallon) was the King of Gwynedd who contracted with Elian upon the saint's return from Rome, and gave him land. The 'cursing ritual' described in the poem, including an inscribed piece of lead or slate, a wooden bowl and repeated imprecations, was an accurate representation of the ceremonies described in connection with Ffynnon Elian at the first trial, which took place in 1818, a few years after the poem was published. The traditional, iconic, elements of 'cursing', the 'Hag' and her 'charm', would have been familiar to all readers of fairy tales, Gothic novels and Romantic literature, but the 'wooden bowl' and the 'lead tablets' suggest that Miss Wardle had an unexpectedly detailed knowledge of the rituals at Ffynnon Elian.

And possibly she had. Gwilym Lloyd Wardle (1762 – 1833) bought the Wern Estate at Penmorfa on the Lleyn peninsula in 1802, and lived there with his family including daughter Charlotte.[9] Within two miles of the Wern Estate the Rev. Jeoffrey Holland, estranged husband of Margaret Holland the first known 'priestess' of Ffynnon Elian, was ensconced as the rector of Dolbenmaen Penmorfa. And within a mile of Wern was Tan-yr-allt, where Percy Bysshe Shelley lived for two years between 1811 and 1813, presumably the time that Charlotte Wardle was writing 'St Aelian's Well'. It is tempting to imagine the young poet Charlotte Wardle, the local rector Jeoffrey Holland and possibly Shelley himself, in the warmth and light of candle-lit winter evenings around a crackling fire at Wern, listening to Jeoffrey Holland's stories about Ffynnon Elian, 'the Cursing Well' and his former wife, Margaret, the 'priestess'. What is more likely is that Ffynnon Elian, 'the Cursing Well', had become very well-known indeed in North Wales by the end of the first decade of the 19th century and the young poet's imagination had responded accordingly.

Charlotte Wardle's intended audience were contemporary Gothic-novel readers and her poem promotes an overblown image of unmitigated evil in the Gothic literary tradition. In the introduction to canto 5, a descriptive note is added:

> The well lies in a dingle near the high road leading from Llan Elian to Groes in Irias, it was surrounded by a wall of six feet high and embosomed in a grove; the trees have fallen and the well thrown down.

Perhaps the well had altered in appearance considerably in the first years of the 19th century although other contemporary accounts indicate that she was using poetic licence to full effect and that Ffynnon Elian in 1812-1814 looked pretty much as it had since the report written for Pennant, with the possible exception of the bathing place, not mentioned again after the 1775 report. Edward Pugh, writing in the first decade of the 19th century and quoted above, described a very different scene to that in 'St Aelian's Well'. In fact, it is not until 1829 that the well was physically destroyed, torn down 'stone by stone'.

---

[9] *Dictionary of Welsh Biography* (London, 1959).

A year after Charlotte Wardle's effusions, in 1815, a book by the Rev. Peter Roberts (1760-1819) was published. In *The Cambrian Popular Antiquities; or, An Account of some Traditions, Customs, and Superstitions, of Wales,* a chapter is devoted to holy wells; St Tegla's, St Dwynwen's, St Elian's, St Winefride's and St Maddern's in Cornwall. These four Welsh wells are considered by Roberts to have been the most important in the country and there are four pages of text on St Elian's well, with suggestions as to its history. Roberts, a scholar and polymath antiquarian who ended his life as the vicar of Halkyn, was both scandalised and impressed by the supposed powers of the well, 'the consequences have frequently been known to be *the death* of the credulous victim.' He described the users of the well as 'the lower orders of the peasantry', and the guardian at the well, as in Wardle's poem, as 'some worthless and infamous wretch, who officiated as priestess.' The process of being 'put in' and 'taken out of' the well is described in some detail, and he mentions, as others before him, a 'book' containing the names of those who are 'cursed', with names in it that are only erased when they have duly paid to have the curse removed. Rev. Roberts, like other Anglican clergy, was troubled by Ffynnon Elian's reputation for cursing and expressed clearly the Protestant desire to stamp out all forms of 'superstitious practice' that he interpreted as lingering Catholic observance and pagan behaviours. He was, however, unique in questioning the assertion that for a holy well to be used solely for cursing was credible, noting:

> That a well should be dedicated even to a popish saint, as a well of cursing, or as a means of satiating a diabolical spirit of revenge, even with every allowance for the uncharitable spirit of popery, is not credible.

He then contributed his own theory:

> The superstition must, therefore, be considered as Druidical; and, it is most probable, that this well was originally dedicated to *Malaen*, the genius of destruction, who is represented as a fury; that it was called at first Ffynnon Malaen; and the monks, finding it difficult to eradicate the custom, and wishing to suppress a Druidic appellation, substituted *Aelian* for *Malaen*.

No Welsh word approximating to 'Malaen' can be found, although the English homonym 'malign' makes the meaning clear enough.

The first court case, 1818

Margaret Holland died in 1810, and Cefn-y-Ffynnon farm, still owned by the Royle family, was let to farmer Robert Jones and his wife, of Glan yr afon, Betws-yn-Rhos, a few miles from Llanelian. They became 'guardians' of the well and it was during their time at Cefn-y-Ffynnon that the first court case concerning Ffynnon Elian was heard in the Flintshire Great Sessions of 1818. The depositions taken from four visitors to the well at that time, given in connection with the court case, provide a detailed account of ritual at Ffynnon Elian and reasons for going there.

The court case concerned an accusation of fraud, brought by Edward Pierce of Llandyrnog (nearly 25 miles away from Llanelian) against John Edwards, from Northop (45 miles away). Edwards had promised Pierce that he could 'take him out' of Ffynnon Elian, and thus improve his health. They came to the well and various rituals took place, but the promised return to health did not materialise, and Pierce sued for fraud. John Edwards had no connection with the well, no magical powers, nor did he claim any. He claimed only to be able to 'take Pierce out' of the well, on payment of fourteen shillings and sixpence and with this claim the essential promise of Ffynnon Elian is made clear. By being 'taken out' of the well (*whether or not* one had ever been 'put in' it), a 'curse' could be removed and relief from any anxiety or affliction obtained.

Edwards was convicted of fraud, narrowly escaped transportation and was sentenced to twelve months in jail. The depositions connected with the case were taken in Caernarfonshire (no addresses are given) and used in evidence during the court hearing. The three deponents who gave evidence were Richard Pugh, William Owen and William Roberts. They all described their reasons for using Ffynnon Elian and gave their evidence on oath. Their dictated statements were read in court. (The handwriting is in the same hand for each one). Richard Pugh wanted to ascertain whether or not his brother's name was 'in the well'. William Owen had come to see if a 'G. Roberts' had been put in the well. William Roberts' wife was ill, and he had come to see if her initials were in the well.

For anyone to be 'in the well', their initials carved into slate or stone had to be found in the well, or in the farmhouse. Stones or slates with initials on them were kept 'in a hat' in an upstairs room at Cefn-y-Ffynnon, or were to be found in a large wooden bowl balanced over the inner well and filled with marked slates. The names of those who had been 'put in' the well were also to be found in a book in the farmhouse. The guardians obviously kept a large number of slates with every possible combination of initials on them. It was a fool-proof method of ensuring that anyone who came to Ffynnon Elian could be 'taken out' of the well (and that their income was protected).

The ritual described by all three deponents involved walking around the inner well that was surrounded by a high stone wall and a lockable door, indicating that in 1818 the structure described for Pennant in the report of 1775 and by Edward Pugh in *Cambria Depicta*, 35 or so years later, was still standing albeit with the addition of a 'lockable door'. Water was thrown over the petitioners' heads by the *offeiriad* (priest), words from the psalms were spoken and then, inside the well-house at the inner well the water was checked to see if it 'sparkled' or not. The slate or stone with the initials of the person who was to be 'taken out' of the well was then taken out of the bowl and given to the petitioner to take away.

The deponents wanted a loved one 'taken out' of the well to relieve illness or another tragic circumstance and it is clear that by the second decade of the 19th century Ffynnon Elian still inspired the belief that what felt like a curse could be lifted by a visit to the well. Life in North Wales in 1818 was full of curses. Poverty was a principal curse as the price of corn had risen steadily since the beginning of the 19th century and was at its highest after the Napoleonic Wars. The continuing loss of common land restricted the poorer families' ability to provide food for themselves and thus retain a degree of independence. Illness with no money to pay for the medical care that was available was another curse. Then there was the desperate problem of how to support a family if the breadwinner had not returned from the war, or was incapacitated and not able to do the heavy mining or agricultural work that was available. The cost of a visit to Ffynnon Elian must have represented a serious challenge to most families but the potential rewards must equally have seemed to be worth it. These were some of the reasons for even considering a visit to Ffynnon Elian, reasons that must have included an extremity of fear, despair and hope.

Richard Pugh paid the woman at the well (Mrs Jones, the wife of the tenant Robert Jones) 12 shillings, plus another 2 shillings thrown directly into the well. William Owen paid 10 shillings plus another one shilling thrown into the well and William Roberts paid 12 shillings also, plus another one for the well. A fourth deponent who contributed briefly to the court case was the daughter of John Hughes of Llanfairfechan (fifteen miles away), and in her deposition she stated, presumably after an argument about the charges, that 'the man or woman said that they had very little means to pay their rent, the land being so poor, but from the profits arising from the well'. Mr and Mrs Jones may have needed the money from Ffynnon Elian to pay their rent but any one of these charges for a session at the well represented a sizeable income. By 1810, labourers in North Wales were earning 1 shilling and sixpence to 2 shillings a day. Wages were never stable, and went down over the next decades as the aftermath of the Napoleonic Wars took its economic toll. Costs at Ffynnon Elian changed also. Edward Pierce paid John Edwards 14 shillings and sixpence in 1818 to be 'taken out' of the well. By the time of the second court case connected with Ffynnon Elian, in 1831, the cost of being 'taken out' of the well had gone down to 7 shillings.

References to the Ffynnon Elian court case of 1818 appeared afterwards in nationally distributed magazines, as well as in local newspapers. In 1822, *The Cambro-Briton* included a lengthy footnote about Elian in their glossary of saints' names. They reported the court case in detail, and concluded, 'This trial affords as extraordinary an instance, as any on record, of ignorant and superstitious credulity, and is more worthy of the monkish ages than of the nineteenth century.'

The strongest reaction to the court case was published in 1823, five years after it was over. This was an anonymous magazine article published in *The Album*. The case was retold and enlivened still further with fictitious names and personalities ('Jones was a surly, gloomy, envious fellow') and referred to the 'proprietress' (the farmer's wife Mrs Jones) as the 'Cursing Hag of the well.' The protagonists in the court case are described as 'farmers' in the article, although the actual professions of John Edwards and Edward Pierce are not mentioned in any newspaper account. According to *The Album*, 'farmer Lloyd' is cursed by 'farmer Jones' that he 'might be seized by a consuming malady, which should, ere long, terminate in death, and that he might die *standing*'. 'This story is true' insists the anonymous author, 'the names of Jones and Lloyd are fictitious. This example is selected…[as] I am well acquainted with the minute particulars attending it'. The author deploys his views on the Welsh as further proof of the evil nature of the well:

> The man whose heart is set on cursing his fellow-creature, thinks a walk of twenty, thirty, or even forty miles, a trifling exertion, compared to the gratification of seeing a hated neighbour pine gradually away...It is difficult to believe that so fiend-like a spirit can inhabit a human bosom, or pollute a Christian land; but it is a fact, that numbers of ill-tempered, implacable Welshmen walk many miles every year, for the purpose of cursing him whom Christ commanded us to forgive, though he should offend us, not seven times only, but seventy times seven.

At the end of the lengthy article, the author concludes with the observation that:

> In consequence of a trial of which Fynnon Aelian, or the Well of Aelian was the subject, the justices of the peace for the county of Denbigh met to consult on the means of ridding the country of this disgraceful evil; according to their sentence, the well was choked up with rubbish, and its ancient proprietess prosecuted.

This description is inaccurate in every way. It has not been possible to find evidence of court proceedings having been brought against any 'woman of the well', and Ffynnon Elian continued to attract visitors for several more decades. The description of the well as 'choked up with rubbish' may refer to a time after 1818 but is contradicted by the depositions that describe Ffynnon Elian as having a high stone wall and a lockable door. The 'proprietress' was tenant Robert Jones' wife, as Margaret Holland had died eight years earlier. That such an inaccurate and derogatory article should have been published at all reflects the commonly held contemporary prejudice of the English towards the Welsh, who were often ridiculed in popular magazines and portrayed as a primitive, ignorant, superstitious people who, as we see here and elsewhere, had no moral compass.

Also in 1823 *The Edinburgh Magazine* published an article on the popular superstitions of the Welsh. In the opening sentence a now-familiar note is struck:

> The Welsh peasantry are a highly superstitious people: living, as they do, in so rude and secluded a country, their very being is incorporated with divers strange phantasies.

The article included a report on the court case at Ffynnon Elian copied in its entirety from *The Cambro-Briton* of the previous year. *The Edinburgh Magazine* also contained a lengthy footnote on the mode of cursing at the well, the 'worthless and infamous' woman of the well, the book in which the names were kept of those who had been cursed and the pin used in the ceremony of cursing. The results of being 'put into the well', according to the writer, were that:

> If the individual were a person of credulous disposition, the idea, like that of the Indian Obi soon preyed upon his spirits and the poor unhappy object pined himself to death, unless a timely reconciliation should take place between the parties.

The suggestion of foreign witchcraft practices was copied in *The Retrospective Review* of 1825. In describing the effect of being 'put in the well' the writer suggested that 'if the individual were cursed with a credulous disposition, the idea, like that of the West Indian Obi, soon preyed upon his spirits, and at length terminated in his destruction.' The article was reprinted once more in 1837, in *The Saturday Review*. In this later version, details of the court case of 1831 were included.

There is no mention of a 'curse' having been put on anyone connected with the court case in 1818. John Edwards is accused of fraud, because he hoped that his friend Edward Pierce would improve in health, and that he, John Edwards, would get the credit for it, and some money into the bargain. The statements from all the deponents made it clear that they visited Ffynnon Elian to have a curse that was not necessarily of attributable human agency, lifted from someone they loved.

The insistence by these writers on the evil nature of all transactions at Ffynnon Elian can be put down to the desire for a sensational 'story' based on accepted prejudices (and a lack of inclination to do any research), but the mention of 'Obi' is an additional illustration of a widely-held belief in the essential 'foreignness' of the Welsh. The association of the practices at Ffynnon Elian with the magic of another culture ('West Indian Obi'), highlights the way in which the Welsh were seen as 'other' by writers for the English reading market.

'Obeah' or 'Obeye' is described as having a dualistic nature. It is the belief that one can use certain spirits or supernatural agents to work harm to the living, or to call them off from such mischief. In the 19th century, the British used the term 'Obeah' to describe all slave acts and practices that were considered supernatural or evil in nature, such as rituals and fetishes. It is noteworthy that the home-grown witchcraft practices of the British Isles are not mentioned in connection with Ffynnon Elian in any publication during the 18th, 19th or 20th centuries. 'Obi' is a very foreign concept indeed, and its use in connection with Ffynnon Elian reinforced a cultural separation between Wales and England that was obviously acceptable to the English reading public. The article comparing Obeah and Ffynnon Elian was reprinted twice, doubly emphasising the potency of Ffynnon Elian, and its paralysing effect upon the will.

At the end of the 1820s, Ffynnon Elian began to interest antiquarian writers. In *The Cambrian Quarterly Magazine and Celtic Repertory* (London, 1829), H. Hughes writes in his introduction to an article on superstition, 'Ah! is there one so profane as to smile at our serious assertion? We will forthwith "put him in St. Elian's Well". He knows not, probably, the import of this threat: he shall be informed anon'. Stories about the well were not (Hughes writes):

> …amusing fables…but the actual creed of a peasantry sober and phlegmatic… repeated in the cottage as…matters of credence and certainty. We do not expect this simplicity of understanding to continue long among our cottagers. The increased communication between them and their *Saesneg* [English] neighbours, together with their Sunday-schools and parish libraries will… cause the superstitions of …the time past… to become as a tale that is told. [this] present opportunity is, probably, the last that will be afforded for the preservation of their memory.

The desire to record and cherish the 'superstitions of the time past' struck a new note, and the antiquarian writers of the rest of the 19th century continued to find Ffynnon Elian an interesting and rewarding topic. In 1824 another detailed record of the 1818 court case was reported in a London magazine. No comment was added to the testimony of those who appeared in court, and the article appeared under the heading of 'Hoaxes and Impostures', creating the impression that the whole affair was a light-hearted joke. The 1818 court case had run its course as journalistic fodder for English magazines.

But how was Ffynnon Elian perceived by the local Welsh community during these early years of the 19th century? From the end of the 18th century a wave of Welsh-speaking, religious and cultural force had swept up from the South and was making itself felt in North Wales. Nonconformist chapels of all denominations were being built and local feeling about Ffynnon Elian was about to intensify once more.

Ffynnon Elian, the Nonconformist movement and Capel Nant Meifod

In the same year as the last English magazine article about the 1818 court case, 1824, a winning poetic entry in the Eisteddfod Genedlaethol (National Eisteddfod) was by Edward Jones. The title, 'Can a'r ffolineb swyngyfaredd, a phob ofergoelion eraill' (Poem on foolishness of spells and all other superstitions), warns that superstitious behaviour goes against God's law. Ffynnon Elian is used as a warning to men wanting wealth and power, 'trwy i Ffynnon, i'w danfon y dew' (through the well, men wanted to prosper), and is used as an example to others of the terrible results of belief in superstitious practices. Edward Jones (1761-1836) was a poet, farmer and schoolmaster from Llanrhaeadr Dyffryn Clwyd, approximately 20 miles from Llanelian. He was a Calvinistic Methodist who had 17 children and left a small body of poetry and three hymns still used in the Methodist hymnal. His concerns about the well were fervently supported by the Methodists who settled, proselytised and changed the religious face of this small corner of North Wales.

'Welsh Methodism', writes Geraint H. Jenkins, 'was a 'heart-religion',[10] and its fervent adherents were determined and forceful people who permanently changed the face of religion in Wales. The number of chapels in the landscape eloquently testify to the success of the Nonconformist movement in North Wales although they are now not used as they were in the 19th and 20th centuries. These 'capelau', Independent, Baptist, Presbyterian, Calvinistic and Methodist, were built, attended and cared for by local people and supported by peripatetic preachers, who 'spread the word' as they travelled throughout Wales.

The Nonconformist movement was a response to many factors. Social and political unrest grew and developed into a new nationalism among Welsh speakers, together with a desire for 'spiritual revival' and specifically a desire to worship in Welsh, something that was often not available in the Protestant Church of England in Wales which did not become the Church in Wales until 1922. The Methodists around Llanelian met and worshipped at first at Cilgwyn Farm, home of the Jones family, less than a mile away from Cefn-y-Ffynnon and the well.

---

[10] G.H. Jenkins, *The Foundations of Modern Wales 1642 – 1780* (OUP 1993).

The Methodists who met at Cilgwyn farm formed a group determined to raise their own chapel and to destroy Ffynnon Elian, somewhere they believed promoted a godless belief in satanic powers. They were unshakeable in their belief that theirs was a righteous mission and after they had established themselves at Cilgwyn farm in the late 18th century, they set out not only to destroy belief in the power of Ffynnon Elian to change lives, but to destroy the physical structure of the well itself.

Capel Nant Meifod.

They wrote regularly about their progress to *Y Goleuad* (The Light), the Methodist newspaper, from 1828, while they planned building their chapel, Capel Nant Meifod, and developing their mission along the North Wales coast. *Methodistiaeth yn Nosbarth Colwyn Bay* (A history of the growth of Methodism in Colwyn Bay) summarised their assault on Ffynnon Elian:

> Wedi i'r Methodistiaid gychwyn achos yn y gymydogaeth hon, ac wedi casglu ychydig nerth, un o'r pethau cyntaf a wnaethant ydoedd crynhoi eu galluoedd

yn nghyd i drefnu ymosiad cry far dwyll a honiadaeth Ffynon [sic] Elian.' (After the Methodists founded their group in the neighbourhood and had gathered a little strength one of the first things they did was to summon up their forces to organise a powerful attack on the deception and false claims of Elian's well.)

Two letters to *Y Goleuad*, from 1828, described the efforts of the group to divert would-be supplicants from the well. They met petitioners on the road before they got to Ffynnon Elian, pretended to be the guardians, directed them to another water source and muttered 'mumbo jumbo'. They hoped that as the petitioners failed to achieve their objectives, word would spread that the holy well was a fake and a waste of money and it would close down. When this failed to stop the visitors to Ffynnon Elian (although there is no indication of how many there were at this time), they finally took matters firmly into their own hands. In March 1829, a letter was published in *Y Goleuad* announcing that:

> …yr ydym, gyda mawr hyfrydwch, yn hysbysu i'n cydwladwyr ein bod ni wedi arfer moddion *i lwyr ddileu y Fynnon hono o olwg y byd pechadurus am byth!* Yn y mis diweddaf darfu ni fel gwlad, o un gallon, gyduno i'w chau i fyny, ac fel y canlyn y gwaethom: cloddiasom ffos ddofn o'i hamgylch, a ffos arall oddeutu dwy lath o ddyfnder, yn myned o'f ffos gyntaf un union i'r afon, yr hon sydd o fewn ugain llath i'r ffynnon, yn ngwaelod nant. Rhoddasom y cerig oedd un fur o'i hamgylch yn ngwaelod y ffosydd i gario tan y ddaear i'r afon: a disgwyliwn y bydd cnwd toreithiog o gloron [potatoes] yn tyfu ar y llanerch yr haf nesaf! Yn awr pwy bynag fyddant mor ynfyd a dyfod at Ffynnon Elian mwy, ni chant ond cyfarth y wal – ni chant ond cais lle bu: a phlant y llan a waeddant ha ha eu hol!!!'

(It is with great pleasure that we inform our fellow countrymen that we have employed a means of completely *eradicating that Well from the sight of the sinful world forever*! In the last month as a country we with one heart agreed together to shut it up, and we did this as follows; we dug a deep ditch around it, and another ditch about two yards in depth, going from the first ditch to the river, which is within twenty yards of the well, at the bottom of a valley. We placed the stones which formed a wall around the well at the bottom of the ditches to carry the stream under the earth to the river. And we anticipate that there will be an excellent potato crop growing on that piece of land next summer.

Now whoever is foolish enough to come to Elian's well again, they can only bark at the wall – they will only find a faint imprint where it was; and the children of the parish will shout Ha! Ha! after them.)

A poem written by one of the congregation and included in the letter begins:

Gorphenwyd cau ar y ffynnon – y dwr

Lle deuai'r ynfidion;

Diles fydd i'r hudolion;

Ni ddaw'r byd o byd i hon.

(The closing down of the well is complete – the water where foolish people used to come. It will be no use to the enchanters, the world will not find it.)

The letter quoted above reveals that there was still a structure for the Methodists to 'tear down' in 1829 and that the well still had an outer and maybe an inner chamber too. Now nothing remains of the outer wall or of any other structure described in the 1775 report, although the 'ditch' dug by the Methodists is still there, connecting the overflow from the well to the stream, Nant Meifod, some yards away. The stones that still lie at the bottom of the ditch may have come from the original well walls. It is also possible that as Capel Nant Meifod was not opened until 1833, the Methodists may have rescued some of the good building blocks from the high walls at Ffynnon Elian and used them to build the walls of their new chapel.

The evils of Ffynnon Elian are the subject of a poem by another Methodist minister, Absolom Roberts (? – 1864). *Lloches Mwyneidd-dra* (The Refuge Of Gentleness), published in 1845, is a collection of *penillion*; poems, songs and hymns set to the harp. Roberts was born in Trefriw on the western side of the River Conwy, nearly 15 miles away from Llanelian, and moved to Eglwysbach, a village 7 miles nearer to Ffynnon Elian, where he lived for 24 years. Absolom Roberts' house in Eglwysbach is reputed to have been the first in that area to attract a regular church meeting. Roberts' songs won first prize in the Eisteddfod in Denbigh in 1828, four years after Edward Jones had won first prize with his poem against the foolishness of superstition. Roberts echoes Edward Jones in these verses:

Near to my dwelling is Saint Elian's well,

Where Satan's servants assemble in widespread wrath;

And great dishonesty,

They're full of folly,

Obstinacy, and (were it enquired into), lies.

They sweep the well, they beg cruelly

For evil upon their neighbours, from the heart, black enmity;

They call the God of heaven,

They abase his name

For that they'll sink like Judas.

And with the Devil to teach them, obedient to please him,

To do as he pleases, where he rules,

And allow them to believe

That there's power in the water,

As long as they disrespect its good owner (i.e. God)

Instead of thanking Him for water lest (they) languish,

(they) use it for enchantment and colour it blue (or green or grey)

To show to men

The great miracle of the old well

And its new, unsuitable tricks.

They resort to it annually for success in worldly wealth,

By the help of the Devil or miserable enchantment;

It's no wonder that in churning,

Their milk stinks,

And they lament, complaining.

Saying that a witch came, on her purpose,

To their house, or their herd, a sorceress full of ire;

Let's all go and enquire

Where the odious she-bear may be

And we'll break her crown with stones

St Elian's well is an old mantle over Satan;

It remains quite complete (but filthy and black)

No one would go near,

If he appeared

Lest they be frightened at dusk

If I were to hear that a cairn of rocks lay

On it, I'd rejoice without ending;

But Satan and his servants

Would bawl cruelly;

Whence went our well, and its purpose (substance?)

Many were sacrificing to the prince of darkness

With no lack of belief, or paying this time;

Oh, miserable creatures,

Doing damage to their own,

And throwing the beloved soul into the well.

A horrible end will come to the keeper of the well;

He does not flee from the midst of Godless fools;

He serves under Satan

He's one in nature

With the devil himself, that I know.[11]

It is likely that these verses were written much earlier than at the time of their publication in Llanrwst, 1845. The mention of an existing keeper of the well indicates that Jac Ffynnon Elian, guardian from about 1820, was *in situ*. 'A horrible end will come to the keeper of the well', writes the author, but he does not mention the court case of 1831. There is still consistent use and no lack of belief in the well at this time, and 'they' are still 'paying'. The members of the Methodist Chapel around the corner from the well had torn down the external structures 'stone by stone' by 1829. These verses, written in the present tense, do not mention this. 'If I were to hear that a cairn of rocks lay on it, I'd rejoice without ending', writes the poet. And also, 'It [the well] remains quite complete [but filthy and black]'. There is a certainty here about contemporary use and the perceived power of the well. This suggests that the poem was written before 1829 and it is likely that it was in fact part of Roberts' Eisteddfod entry for 1828. The Methodists of Capel Nant Meifod would have known of Absolom Roberts in Eglwysbach, a few miles away, and Absolom Roberts would certainly have been one of those who 'rejoiced without ending' when the outer structure of the well was torn down in 1829. That there is no mention in these verses of the efforts of the local Methodists to destroy the 'old mantle over Satan' is another indication that they were written before 1828, and with Edward Jones' winning entry in the Eisteddfod of 1824, it seems that Ffynnon Elian and the need to destroy its powers provided a unifying theme for the early Methodists in North Wales.

Jac Ffynnon Elian and the court case of 1831

Nonconformity and social change accompanying the progression of the 19th century were the reasons that Ffynnon Elian eventually fell into disuse. But despite the proximity of the Methodists' new chapel (Capel Nant Meifod) that opened in 1833 only 20 yards away from Ffynnon Elian, the trickle of visitors to the well and its guardian appears to have continued into the late 1840s. While the outer structures of Ffynnon Elian were being taken down 'stone by stone' by the Methodist congregation, Jac Ffynnon Elian, the last *offeiriad,* remained in his little cottage near

---

[11] Translated by Howard Huws.

the well, named 'Meddiant' (belonging). Meddiant was built on a tiny nib of common land, next to the road between Ffynnon Elian and the Methodist chapel. Possibly Jac had moved into, or re-constructed the remains of the bathing place. He was seemingly powerless to prevent the destruction of the well housing and neither is there any record of the Methodists attacking either Jac's property or his person.

As the final and best-known guardian of the well, John Evans, or Jac Ffynnon Elian as he became known, was a shrewd man who took over what can only be described as a rather precarious 'business opportunity' at Ffynnon Elian. He was born in Llanllechid, near Bangor, in 1791. At the age of ten he came to work at Nant y Glyn farm, a few hundred yards away from Ffynnon Elian. At 13, he was apprenticed to a tailor in Llandrillo-yn-Rhos parish, next to the parish of Llanelian. He knew the area and Ffynnon Elian when Mrs H- (Margaret Holland) was the 'priestess' there. At the time of the first court case in 1818 his name is not mentioned, and it was probably around 1820 that he took up residence in the tiny cottage he had built for himself near to Ffynnon Elian.

We learn about Jac's early life and his tenure as *offeiriad* (priest) at Ffynnon Elian through his autobiography, *Llyfr Ffynon Elian* (The Book of Ffynnon Elian). This was written at some time in the 1850s with the help of William Aubrey, a printer and Baptist from Llanerch-y-Medd in Anglesey. Jac wrote his autobiography after he had become a member of the local Baptist chapel in Llanelian, Capel Ebeneser, that opened its doors in 1831. In his given name of John Evans, Jac chronicled his involvement with Ffynnon Elian, and reflected on his time as *offeiriad* at the well. Ffynnon Elian, as we have seen, provided an income for anyone able to exploit its potential, and Jac Ffynnon Elian grasped his opportunity when it arose with great presence of mind.

His purpose in writing *Llyfr Ffynon Elian,* after he had acted as guardian of the well for probably over 20 years, was twofold. He wanted to impress his readers with his perspicacity and shrewd understanding of human psychology but to also make clear that he was now a reformed character who realised that, 'The work was depraved, and the end of suitable and proper employment for me.' Jac described his introduction to life at Ffynnon Elian as follows, and was suitably candid about his primary motivation for becoming the *offeiriad* at the well:

Daeth y dyn ataf; ac wedi tipyn o siared o gwmpas ac ar hyd, a'i neges yn dyfod yn amlycach i fy meddwl o hyd, gofynodd y dyn i mi o'r diwedd, pwy oedd yn 'edrych ar ol y ffynnon y pryd hwnw!' Dywedais wrtho mai myfi. Meddyliais nad oedd waeth i mi gael yr arian na rhyw yn arall. (A man came along, and I doubted his purpose, and began to think that he had come about the well. After a while he asked who the person was to go to at the well. I said it was me; I thought I might as well have the money as anyone else).

After he had settled down as *offeiriad,* Dic Aberdaron[12], a wandering polyglot, who was known for carrying many books with him and speaking many languages, came to visit him. Jac writes that Dic had the Apocrypha with him, 'Duesyfais un o'r llyfrau ganddo – llyfr yr APPOCRIPHA yn yr iaith CALDAEG oedd hwnnw,' (one of the books he had with him was the Apocrypha, in Chaldean) and Jac writes that the Apocrypha became 'his' book, 'beth bynag y gall fod llyfr rhyw dwyllwr arall'. (whatever other books there may have been for the dark workers).

A Dr Bynian[13] also came to visit Jac, who could 'codi cythreuliaid' (raise devils). He offered Jac valuable advice:

"Gwnaf, siwr," meddai yntau, "Rhowch ar ddeall I'r wlad eich bod yn medru, a daw y wlad I gredu hynny amdanoch ac I briodoli gwyrthiau mawr I chwi. Cymaint a raid I chwi wneyd wedy'n fydd fod yn ddistaw, a chwi a fyddwch yn gystal codwr cythrenliaid a minau, a minau gystal a chwithau" Felly y gwneis, a death y bobol yn fuan I son am danaf ac I ymddiried pob peth I mi, ac I'm harswydo fel pe buaswn yr Arglwydd.

([He] talked a lot about understanding the stars and was able to raise devils, etc. I asked him a lot about the matter, and really wanted to know about the truth of his knowledge. He craved to know more of my ability to raise devils. 'If you let people know you have this knowledge they will come to believe in you, and confer virtue on you' he said to me. So it was done and people soon came after they heard about it, and to confide in me and to be afraid of me as if I were God Almighty.)

---

[12] Born Richard Robert Jones, a native of Aberdaron on the tip of the Llyn peninsula. 1780-1843. He is buried in St Asaph Cathedral churchyard.

[13] A 'magician' from Montgomeryshire, more usually known as 'Doctor Bennion'.

The stories Jac retold in *Llyfr Ffynon Elian* of the visitors to the well and his solutions to their problems never include the use of 'raising devils'. He admits his use of the Apocrypha as part of the ritual at the well but is careful to distance himself from any suggestion of 'magic' of any kind. However, it is highly likely that he used any means at his disposal to protect his income.

He must also have had great confidence in his ability to help people who came to see him. Ffynnon Elian had become notorious as 'the Cursing Well' by the time Jac became the *offeiriad,* and he would have needed great presence of mind to keep his 'business' ticking over in the face of severe local opposition, the ever-present fear of litigation (after the court case of 1818), or more direct personal attack if a disappointed petitioner who had come a long way and paid handsomely, decided to exact retribution.

Jac's decision to become the new *offeiriad* probably coincided with the disappearance of the previous guardians at Ffynnon Elian, the tenant farmer Robert Jones and his family. They had moved away by the early 1820s and the succeeding tenant farmer was a Mr David Jones, one of the first members of the congregation at Capel Nant Meifod. Mr Jones would not have sanctioned anything to do with Ffynnon Elian and his signature is on the letters to *Y Goleuad* quoted above. Jac almost certainly siphoned off the well itself at the same time as he settled into Meddiant, diverting the overflow stream to create a new 'Ffynnon Elian'. No charges of trespass were ever made against him and he continued to live beside the 'new' well and in his own cottage until his death in 1858. He was living at Meddiant with his family during the years that the original Ffynnon Elian was physically destroyed by Methodists.

It is a testament to his skills and understanding of human nature that Jac managed to survive more than ten years as *offeiriad* without any legal action being brought against him. It was not until 1831 that Jac was summoned to the Denbighshire Great Sessions before Judge Baron Bolland and charged with fraud by Elizabeth Davies, who claimed he had taken seven shillings from her and that her husband had not improved in health. Jac in his own defence stated that 'he never sent for anyone to come to the well, nor did he say there was any efficacy in the water, but if a person believed that there was, and chose to give him some money, he took all that they had a mind to give.' The judge gave him a much lighter sentence than had been handed out to John Edwards thirteen years earlier. Baron Bolland, 'after expressing his regret that any person could be found so lamentably ignorant and credulous as to believe that any man, by such ridiculous means, had the power of relieving or controlling the diseases and afflictions of another,' sentenced 'John Evans' (Jac) to six months' hard labour, half the sentence handed out to John Edwards thirteen years previously. Jac served his sentence, and returned to Ffynnon Elian and Meddiant.

After the trial of 1831, another wave of publications about Ffynnon Elian appeared, including one of the more extraordinary responses to the well. Samuel Wilderspin (1792-1866) pioneered teaching methods for infant schools, and founded several hundred schools throughout the United Kingdom. In *Early Discipline Illustrated: or the Infant System Progressing and Successful,* (1840) Wilderspin used Ffynnon Elian as an example of the recalcitrance and resistance of the Welsh to his ideas for reform in the infant school system:

> …all hope of success in Wales was well nigh extinguished. The state of the population, however, appeared to need the greatest exertion. The superstition that prevails almost defies belief…The following will illustrate the state of the *peasantry*.

Wilderspin then devotes four pages to the well of St Elian, outlining the practices in detail and giving a report of the court case brought against Jac Ffynnon Elian. Wilderspin interpreted Jac's success at offering healing and relief at Ffynnon Elian as follows:

> No sooner did he hear of the sickness of any poor person, or of anyone visited by misfortune, than he contrived to let them know their names were in the well, and that nothing could relieve them except they were taken out. Of course, this could not be done without money; and many hundreds of ignorant people were known to travel on foot thirty or forty miles to seek relief; and that in the most distracted state of mind.

He recorded the court case brought against Jac by Elizabeth Davies in minute detail, and ends with his observation that, 'In one respect, however, Wales may be placed in favourable comparison…England and Ireland especially, swarm with beggars.'

Samuel Wilderspin's comments were published shortly before an official commentary on the state of Welsh education (and character). The Royal Commission Report on Education in Wales, known as *Brad y Llyfrau Gleision* (The

Blue Books), was published in 1847 and was being prepared during the 1840s, just after Wilderspin's opinions on early infant education and Ffynnon Elian were published. The Royal Commission Report drew a very unflattering picture of the Welsh, criticising their religious dissent, their morality and their continuing inexplicable desire to use their own language. Wilderspin's comments would have been known to the compilers of the Royal Commission Report and probably warmly applauded.

The last years at Ffynnon Elian.

Wilderspin writes about Ffynnon Elian in the past tense, indicating that he assumed that the well has ceased to attract visitors. From the 1830s Ffynnon Elian became a favourite entry for compilers of the many 'guides', 'dictionaries' and itemised travel journals that were published, and entries are often derivative copies of earlier works. An example is Samuel Lewis, whose *Topographical Dictionary of Wales,* first published in 1833, is an echo of Pennant's *A Tour of Wales,* that had been published more than 50 years earlier:

> In the township of Eirias is the noted well called Ffynnon Elian, which, even in the present age, is annually visited by some hundreds of people, for the reprehensible purpose of invoking curses upon the heads of those who have grievously offended them.

In 1836 the Rev. Rice Rees, in *An Essay on the Welsh Saints* also writes that the well is still active:

> Elian is celebrated in the superstitions of the Principality; miraculous cures were lately supposed to be performed at his shrine at Llanelian, Anglesey; and near to the church of Llanelian, Denbighshire, is a well called Ffynnon Elian, which is thought by the peasantry of the neighbourhood to be endued with miraculous powers even at present.

Interest in Ffynnon Elian had reached America, and the American edition of *The Metropolitan Magazine* of 1836 included a poem about the well of St Elian. Mrs Crawford, the author, assures her readers that 'the good people of ancient Cambria still have the strongest reliance on the efficacy of the saint's "Cursing Well".' However, the third edition of the *Cambrian Travellers Guide* published in 1840 describes the well as, '…formerly in great repute', and in *An Essay on the Character of the Welsh as a Nation in the Present Age*, published in 1841, the author Rev. William Jones writes that the efficacy of the well of St Elian was, '...*till lately*' (author's italics) considered very powerful. Jones was among the first to revel in the past horrors at Ffynnon Elian, now safely over, and once more to erroneously congratulate 'the authorities' for ending visits to Ffynnon Elian:

> How awful it was to mingle religion with such a genuine piece of Satanic work as this! So great were the effects of the curse of the well, on the minds of a great multitude, among the lower ranks, in Gwynedd and Powis, that many have fallen to a premature grave, being terrified to death under the continued apprehension of some awful calamity befalling them. But thanks to the firmness of the magistrates in the neighbourhood, this cause of national disgrace has been wiped away, and at present St. Elian's well yields nothing but a blessing.

A recent publication[14] confirms that Ffynnon Elian was active in 1842, and that Jac Ffynnon Elian was still officiating there. John Evans (Jac) had written to the London Commissioners on 1 July 1842 'humbly' begging for help as he had 'no bread'. He had been 'loading a mangle [that] broke upon me and injured one of my hands and eyes', and if relief was not forthcoming it would be, 'an end to me from hunger.' A month later, the Conway Union replied that the reason they refused assistance to John Evans was that:

> ...he had resorted to his old habits for which he had been formerly prosecuted and punished for obtaining money by imposing upon the credulity of ignorant and superstitious persons who believed in the charms of a celebrated well called 'Ffynnon Elian Well', which some years ago was stopped up by the Magistrates and Justices of the neighbourhood. It is reported that John Evans has received as much as 30s at a time for promising to take their names out [of the well]... the Relieving Officer was also informed that John Evans managed to get money for ale and get drunk.

Business at Jac's well had obviously not been curtailed by the law, even though Jac had tried to resort to the Conway Union for money. It is interesting to note that the price at Ffynnon Elian had now gone up considerably!

---

[14] Chris Draper, *Paupers, Bastards and Lunatics: The State of Conway Workhouse*, 2003

Opinions on whether Ffynnon Elian remained operational or not differed for several more years. In 1846, Ab Ithel[15] wrote in *Archaeologia Cambrensis*:

> This is the most dreadful of all the wells and the one in whose miraculous powers the peasants of the present day most fully believe. Persons who bear any great malice against others, and wish to injure them, frequently resort to the minister of the well…

Parry's New Guide to Wales published in 1848, reported that the business at the well was over. 'Llanelian is celebrated for its cursing well, which, owing to a foolish tradition, was for a long time the terror of the neighbourhood.' The Rev. Robert Williams wrote in 1852, 'Ffynnon Elian…has obtained a sad notoriety as a cursing well among the superstitions of the Welsh peasantry. This melancholy and wicked custom is still continued more or less in spite of the exertions of the neighbouring magistrates, who have frequently convicted the presiding impostor…' *Black's Picturesque Guide Through North and South Wales and Monmouthshire* of 1858 commented that Llanelian was '…celebrated for its holy well, or *Ffynnon Elian*, which, owing to an absurd tradition, was long the terror of the neighbourhood.'

In fact, Jac Ffynnon Elian lived at Meddiant until his death in 1858, aged 67, and continued to act as the *offeiriad* at the well until his conversion to the Baptist faith at some time in the late 1840s or early 1850s. His change of heart was also due to other factors. The railway ran along the coast of North Wales by the 1840s, bringing new people, new industry, new ideas and new opportunities and Cefn-y-Ffynnon farm was sold to the owner of Grwych Castle in 1847.

Jac's conversion was the direct result of a chance meeting with members of the nearby Capel Bedyddwyr Ebeneser (Ebeneser Baptist Chapel). The story of his conversion and baptism into the faith is set out in detail in *Bedyddwyr Cantref y Rhos* (The Baptists of Rhos). John Evans is described as 'y dyn galluog a goleuedig…dyn pell o flaen ei oes oedd,' (He was a clever and enlightened man… in advance of his years). His title and address were given as 'Mr. John Evans, y Meddiant, Offeiriad Ffynnon Llanelian – y Ffynnon y mae iddi fwy o hanes trychinebu na holl ffynhonnau Cymru ynghyd.' (Mr John Evans of Meddiant, priest of the well at Llanelian – the well with the most disastrous history of all the wells in the whole of Wales.) The story begins:

---

[15] Rev. John Williams, perpetual curate of Treuddyn, Mold, used 'Ab Ithel' as his 'bardic' name.

> Un tro death dau genad o Fon i gasglu at Capel Bucarneddi. Ac wedi yr aethant yng nghfeiriad Llanelian, heibio Croes-yn Eirias, goddiweddwyd hwy gan storm enbyd o wlaw a tharanau. Gan fod y tywyllwch hefyd yn eu dal penderfynesant dioi i'r ty cyntaf a gaent i ofyn lloches tros nos. Y ty cyntaf y daethant iddo oedd Meddiant. (Two men from Anglesey were meeting at Capel Bucarneddi. When they got to Groes-yn-Eirias, near Llanelian, a terrible storm broke out and they decided to ask for shelter overnight at the first house they came to. That house was Meddiant.)

The wife at the house was 'yn barchus iawn' (very respectable) and offered a bed for the night. After supper and before bed, the men read from the Bible and prayed for mercy for sinners. This had the required effect on John Evans and, 'Hydref 17, 1853, bedyddiwyd e far broffes o'i ffydd yng Nghrist, gan y Parch, J. J. Williams.' (He was baptised on 17 October 1853, and professed his faith in Christ, with preacher J. J. Williams.) He was persuaded to write about his life at the well rather than continue to officiate there, and he collaborated with William Aubrey on *Llyfr Ffynon Elian* at some time between his conversion and whenever the book was published, probably after his death in 1858. He is buried in the churchyard of Capel Ebeneser, in the village of Llanelian. His given name, John Evans, is on the tombstone with his address, Meddiant.

After Jac Ffynnon Elian quit his life as an *offeiriad* to join the local Baptist chapel, no one followed in his footsteps. Cefn-y-Ffynnon (and Ffynnon Elian as part of the property) was sold by the Royle family on 16 April 1847 for £1,970.00 at public auction, to Lloyd Hesketh Bamford Hesketh Esq, of Gwrych Castle, in Abergele, some six miles away. By then the slate, copper and stone mining industries were booming in North Wales, as were tourism and agriculture, and the severe hardships of the early years of the nineteenth century, exacerbated by the Napoleonic Wars, were over.

However, Ffynnon Elian continued to be of great interest to antiquarians, to local historians and folklorists and continued to be written about extensively. In 1881 a guide book, *The Gossiping Guide to Wales,* reported:

> Ffynnon Elian, which seems to have been every whit as great a curse as ever St. Winefrides was a blessing to Welsh humanity…the tales told of it have filled one and would fill twenty volumes…we have ourselves met people who not only believed in the well, but also believed they had been "put in it".

More formal texts also mentioned the well. In 1870, in the one-volume edition of *The History of the Diocese of St Asaph*, Archdeacon D.R. Thomas included this footnote: 'I have myself known a well-to-do farmer in a former parish who lost £80 rather than ask for it back again, for fear of being put into the well, and I have met with a person in England pining away to death under the belief that she had been so cursed'. In 1914, the Royal Commission of Ancient and Historic Monuments reported that, 'The well has been filled up, and has practically disappeared, save that the old cobbled pathway is still visible.' A note underneath the entry includes this anecdote:

> Many years ago the Inspecting Officer was told by a very aged and intelligent gentleman of Wrexham that he remembered his father journeying on horseback to the well of St. Elian to consult the priest of the well in the matter of a theft.'

Stories about the well.

Jac Ffynnon Elian's autobiography, *Llyfr Ffynon Elian,* contains the history of his relationship with Ffynnon Elian, ten stories about the well, letters of thanks from satisfied 'customers' and an interview with William Aubrey, his publisher. Throughout the text Jac is called by his given name, John Evans, to distance him from 'Jac Ffynnon Elian' the *persona* that was cast aside when Jac joined the Baptist church. The narratives are presented as moral fables, written from the point of view of a reformed penitent. They are designed to reward the reader for having the sophistication to distance himself from the transactions at the well whilst enjoying the skill and judgement of the guardians (Mrs M. H- and Jac himself). William Aubrey the publisher judged his audience well and *Llyfr Ffynon Elian* was a modest success. In 1861, H. Humphreys of Caernarfon reprinted and serialised the stories and extracts from *Llyfr Ffynon Elian* in *Llyfr Gwybodaeth Gyffredinol* (a Book of Common Knowledge) and Aubrey also retold the stories in his *Llyfrau Ceiniog* (Penny Books).

Jac explained the power of Ffynnon Elian and the longevity of the well's successful active life in terms of man's responsibility for his own feelings and his own destiny. This essentially secular sentiment is familiar to contemporary readers and the power of the 'placebo' effect in use in medicine today. It is interesting to come across it expressed so clearly in mid-19th century rural Wales:

> Peth mawr ydy anghrediniaeth, a pheth mawr ydw ffydd. Y mae dylanwad meddwl dyn arno ei hun un fywyd ac angau iddo ar lawer tro, felly yr oedd gyda hwn. (Unbelief is a huge thing, as is faith. Man's effect upon himself is often a matter of life and death.)

There are nine stories in *Llyfr Ffynon Elian* from Jac's time as guardian of Ffynnon Elian which began around 1820, and one from an earlier time when 'Mrs H-' (Margaret Holland) was the 'Priestess' at the well. Jac had been living near Ffynnon Elian since 1804 when he came to work on a nearby farm in his early teens. He may have known 'Mrs H-' quite well. The narratives involve, among others, a farmer from Caernarfon, a gentleman from Liverpool, a shopkeeper's wife from Abergele, a young man from South Wales, two women from Colwyn Bay, a drover from Anglesey and a miner from Flint.

'Troion Trwstan' (Sad Times) is the earliest story, from the time when Margaret Holland was the guardian of the well. 'Mrs H – gwraig pur barchus, yn byw mewn le mawr, oedd Offeiriadyddes y Ffynon y pryd hwn,' (Mrs H-, a respectable woman, living in the big house,[16] was the priestess of the well at that time.) A young wife came from Caernarfon to ask St Elian to ensure that her elderly husband became blind. She wanted to continue her relationship with a young tailor, but not to jeopardise her comfortable home. Her husband, warned of her deception, arrived at Cefn-y-Ffynnon first, begging Mrs H- not to listen to his young wife. Mrs H- put him into a cupboard so that he could hear what his young wife asked when she arrived, and charged the young wife five guineas for her consultation. When the young wife had left after making her request Mrs H- suggested that the old man should pretend to be blind at home that night and when he was fairly sure that the young wife believed him, wait for her to rendezvous with her young lover, before taking a whip to the young man. They returned home and as Mrs H- suggested the husband pretended to be blind and the young wife and her lover met, only to be faced with the wrath of the outraged husband. 'Cyn hir, beth bynnag, cafodd y teiliwr fyned ymaith wrth grefu ei hun am fyned, a'r wraig fyned ymaith wrth grefu am beidio'. (Before long the tailor was allowed to go away as he wanted and the young wife was sent away as she pleaded not to be.) Here the would-be 'punisher' is punished, suitably chastised for her desire to keep her husband and her young lover.

---
[16] This was presumably Cefn-y-Ffynnon farmhouse.

The young wife may have come to put a curse her husband, but human agency has ensured that 'natural justice' is done.

'Llangc eisau lladd ei dad' (the young man who wanted to kill his father) is the tale of a young man whose *cariad* (sweetheart) wanted to be married but who would not go to live at his farm after they married while the father was still living there. The young man didn't want to leave his home because he was afraid his father would leave the farm, the young man's inheritance, to someone else. They had been courting for 12 years and the young woman had caught the eye of another young man. The subject of the story came to Ffynnon Elian from 'Y Gelli' (Hay-on-Wye) in order to ask for the death of his father, so he could keep his farm and marry his sweetheart. The nature of his request reached the village of Llanelian via local inhabitants before he arrived from the well to find shelter for the night. He spent the evening in the local pub and the men of the village attacked him when they heard his story:

> Fel yr oedd y ddiod yn codi i'w pennau, yr oedd eu ffyrnigrwydd yn codi i'w ganlyn, ac wrth feddwl am ei dad ei hun, methodd rhyw langc a dal – dechreuodd ymosod ar yr hwntw. (As the beer went to their heads, the anger grew fiercer. Thinking about his own father, one young man attacked the South Walian, and the rest followed suit.)

The young man went home beaten and found that his father had discovered where he had gone, would not speak to him and died soon afterwards, having made arrangements to leave the farm to someone else. His sweetheart married her other suitor.

Three stories, 'The Gentleman from England', 'A Woman from Abergele', and 'A Farmer's Wife' illustrate that relief from the anxiety that they *had* been cursed was the predominant reason for a visit to Ffynnon Elian. Jac relieved their anxiety differently in each case, stressing that their worries were quite unfounded. The farmer's wife came to stay with him and daily washing in well water and long walks convinced her she was better. The woman from Abergele refused to believe that she had not been 'put in' the well, and returned many times until Jac produced a pebble with her initials on it and she then felt better. The 'gentleman' from Liverpool, unable to walk, read the eighth psalm for three nights and put a fistful of salt in the fire in his lodgings at the same time. Jac went some of his way home with him, and the gentleman had recovered by the time he returned to Liverpool. He came back often to see Jac, and to pay to keep himself in good health. Jac's comments on the 'gentleman from Liverpool', quoted below, are repeated throughout the text of *Llyfr Ffynon Elian*; illness of mind and body can only be cured by a change of mind in the sufferer:

> Cyn dyfod yma yr oedd yn credu ei fod yn y ffynnon, a chan ei fod yno, mai ofer oedd pob *physic* a dyfais dynol er ei iachau; ac mewn gwirionedd felly yr oedd. Nid oedd dim ar gorff y dyn ond yr afiechyd yr oedd ei feddwl wedi ei ddylanwadu iddo. A phan y credodd hwnw ei ddylanwad yr un fath, a mendiodd. (Before he came here he believed he was under the well's curse, and that being so, all medicine was no use. There was nothing wrong with his body except what the mind had created for it. When he believed the cause of the affliction had been disposed of, it had an effect on him and he recovered.)

'Peckaid Gwenith' (A peck of grain) concerns theft. Two women used the same mill and the same *popty* (bakery) to grind their grain and make their bread, but flour was missing and the women accused the miller. He suggested a visit to Ffynnon Elian, and the two women accompanied the miller to visit Jac. Jac considered the case, noticed that one of the woman looked uneasy, and then pronounced that a woman has stolen the grain and is in deep trouble, '…ac y mae hi wedi ei gwneyd yn ddiffrwyth o'i gwasg i lawr, druan, pwy bynag ydi hi.' (…and the poor woman has been made barren from the waist down, whoever she may be.) The thief, Neli, immediately cried, confessed and begged to be restored, and Jac, after performing several rituals designed to frighten her, asked for payment and then she was free.

In his life as Jac Ffynnon Elian, John Evans describes the use of what we might now describe as 'just' common sense and attention to detail. An example of this is 'Y Wraig a Gollodd y Gwyddau' (The Wife who Lost the Geese). After she had come to visit Jac, who was found 'ar y bwrdd gartref yn gweithio…teiliwr ydoedd o ran ei grefft' (working at a table at home… he was a tailor by trade) she asked for help to find the thief who stole her geese. Jac made his room as dark as possible, found a picture of a man with some geese and a pig in a farming magazine, and told the woman that she would see the face of the thief when he very briefly showed her a picture of him. He lit a small candle, briefly showed her the picture before whisking it away and '…rhoes screech ofnadwy – neidiodd yn ei hol gan waeddi… 'Shion Ty'n-y-Gamdda o dyna fo; adwaenis ei hen wep o yn y munud'; (she gave a dreadful shriek and jumped back, exclaiming, 'It's Sion Ty'n-y-Gamdda, I knew his old face immediately!')

More tales of Ffynnon Elian are reported by the antiquarian cleric Rev. Elias Owen (1833-1899). He was preparing a book entitled *The Holy Wells of North Wales* when he died at home in May 1899 and his unfinished manuscript is in the National Library of Wales. Owen had published *Welsh Folk-Lore, A Collection of the Folk-Tales and Legends of North Wales* in 1888, funded by 200 subscribers who recognised his depth of interest and knowledge of Welsh folk-lore. He edited and contributed to several local and national history publications and travelled from parish to parish in North Wales in his role as Official Inspector of Church of England schools. He sought out the oldest inhabitants of every village he came to and recorded their memories of past stories and legends. He was very interested in Ffynnon Elian and visited it several times, noting that 'The well and its surroundings present a deserted appearance.' In 1890 he drew a map of the site, based on conversations he had with 'An aged woman, who knew personally the last custodian, the spot on which his house stood, and the position of the well'.

In his unfinished and unpublished manuscript[17] he writes that 'Innumerable tales are related in connection with Ffynnon Elian' and that he 'has collected quite a number'. He retells eight tales, and may have recorded many more had he lived to finish his work. Several are also to be found in *Llyfr Ffynon Elian*. Of the remainder, two of Owen's tales concern animals, one a sow who was the 'four leggged thief' that stole her owner's corn. She died after her owner had been to the well to curse the thief. 'A dog placed in the well' was told to Owen by Mrs Wynne of Coed Coch, Dolwen, Betws-yn-Rhos, a member of the local gentry. A young relative of Mrs Wynne, after being told about Ffynnon Elian, had written the name of a favourite dog, Moustache, on a piece of paper, and put it into the well. The dog had been run over by the time the Wynnes' carriage returned home.

'A woman cursed at St Elian's well' is a report of the effect on a woman of believing that she had been cursed at Ffynnon Elian. Owen was visiting Dolanog, Montgomeryshire when he met a man whose sister believed she had been cursed at St Elian's Well and was doomed to remain in bed as long as the woman who had cursed her was alive. On a later visit, Owen was told that with the death of the

---

[17] National Library of Wales 3290D.

woman who was believed to have placed the curse the victim was able to get out of bed.

These three tales do not mention the intervention of a guardian and lack the redemptive nature of the tales recounted by Aubrey, thirty years earlier. A fourth tale, collected by Owen but not included in *Llyfr Ffynon Elian*, 'A young woman and her husband', does include the intervention of Jac Ffynnon Elian, and the psychological expertise that characterised so many of the stories connected with him. A young woman complained to Jac that she could not get along with her husband, with whom she rowed constantly. Jac gave her a bottle of the water from Ffynnon Elian and told her to take a mouthful and hold it in her mouth until her husband had stopped speaking. She complained that the water would run out almost immediately, and Jac advised her to fill the bottle with ordinary water whenever she took a mouthful, so that there would always be a drop of water from Ffynnon Elian in the bottle. She returned to see him a few months later and declared that she was now 'the happiest of women'.

After Jac died in 1858, interest in the well did not die with him. Articles in antiquarian, historical and folklore journals have appeared steadily since then but the reputation for cursing that was established by the early decades of the 19th century remains dominant. The longevity and depth of belief in Ffynnon Elian's complex powers to grant wishes of any kind, to harm and to heal, has remained unacknowledged. Ffynnon Elian clearly provided the hope of a successful solution to any and all of life's difficulties, and as such was resorted to until Jac Ffynnon Elian yielded to religious pressures of the mid-19th century, not legal pressure as was stated so confidently, so often.

He and the other guardians can perhaps be most accurately described as 'wise' men and women, or 'cunning-folk' as Owen Davies calls them,[18] people who 'provided explanations and solutions for the many misfortunes that occurred in their daily lives, as well as holding out the prospect of a better future through the attainment of love and money.' Cunning-folk are not associated with religion of any kind, nor traditionally with holy wells, and the narratives related by Jac Ffynnon Elian and other sources do not specifically mention what Owen Davies describes as the cunning-folk's 'bread and butter', healing the bewitched. Cursing is not mentioned

---

[18] *Popular Magic: Cunning-folk in English History*. 2007.

in Davies' text, although it can be argued that to believe one has been 'bewitched' or that one has been 'cursed' are comparable states of mind.

There is a notable absence of charms, bewitching and other familiar magical terminology in connection with the authentically documented ritual at Ffynnon Elian, although those who wrote about the well without visiting supplied a full repertoire. The rituals recorded by the deponents in the 1818 court case include the speaking of some religious verses, often from the Apocrypha or the Psalms, traversing the area around the well 3 times and the use of the water from a holy well as the medium through which an individual's name on a tablet, slate or stone can be passed to another dimension.

It cannot be said that the practices at Ffynnon Elian were without parallel among wells in the British Isles although the available evidence indicates that this was indeed the only well in the 18th and 19th centuries to have had a reputation for cursing. Other holy wells in Wales and in the rest of Britain are known to have been able to grant wishes of all kinds, without being known as 'cursing wells'. Seeking vengeance, restoration of lost property, advice on relationships and medical help were all reasons for visiting Ffynnon Elian. At one stage the holy well also disturbed the social order, although there is little evidence that this was a common, or frequent use. During the time of the Napoleonic Wars and immediately afterwards, when the smallest wrongdoing or trivial theft was punished severely whatever the desperate circumstances, Ffynnon Elian appears to have been used successfully as a threat to avoid prosecution. Fear of being 'put in' the well scared the landowner who would have otherwise prosecuted the 'turnep' stealer for the loss of a few vegetables. The well was also used to frighten the local children into good behaviour, something that is still remembered in the locality.

In the recorded stories connected with Ffynnon Elian the power of the well is only accessible through a human medium. A 'woman at the well', a 'priestess', a 'guardian' or *offeiriad*, are part of almost every tale. This is distinctive among holy well use, although 'caretakers' are mentioned in connection with other wells, and the larger holy wells would of course have needed care and protection. At Ffynnon Elian, however, they seem to have been a vital part of the ritual at the well rather than just cleaners. And they were paid for their services.

That Ffynnon Elian became known as 'the Cursing Well' despite its clearly stated complexity of use in 1775 has been seen to be the result of publications appearing from the end of the 18th century, beginning with Pennant and the threat made against him. The suggestion that Welsh people kept returning to the well in order to express their hatred of one another was promoted vigorously in English magazines. Ffynnon Elian, 'the Cursing Well', embodied the superstitious, primitive and foreign image of Wales that was acceptable in the England of the early 19th century.

Welsh Nonconformists were contemptuous of what they considered the godless Satan-worship involved in the transactions at the well and destroyed the well structures but they never characterised Ffynnon Elian as 'the Cursing Well'. Jac was received into the Baptist faith where his understanding and skill were recognised and acknowledged. The testimony of Jac Ffynnon Elian, the depositions taken in Caernarfonshire and other sources reviewed here indicate that the petitioners at the well came primarily to *remove* the 'curses' of painful realities, rather than to add to them, and were willing to pay to do this. *Llyfr Ffynon Elian,* Jac's autobriography, presents Jac as John Evans, the servant of those in need, rather than a skilful manipulator of the woebegone who was only interested in his own financial gain. There can be little doubt that Jac was both and that he made money out of the fears and frailties of the people who came to him. *Llyfr Ffynon Elian* neatly sidestepped Jac's culpability and celebrated his successes. William Aubrey, Baptist and printer of Llanerch-y-Medd, has produced a fascinating portrait of a reformed sinner who embodied a psychological understanding of human beings. Aubrey also recognised the potential financial reward from Jac's story, and his tales of the well were re-printed in Welsh-language magazines and newspapers throughout the late 19th century.

It must be acknowledged that Jac was able to help at least some of those who trusted him and believed in the power of St Elian to grant their wishes with his help. Ffynnon Elian's longevity of use is evidence for this. Jac's remarkable understanding of his effect on troubled people and the continuing use of Ffynnon Elian into the Victorian era, long after the time when such seemingly anachronistic practices were thought to have ended, bears witness to that understanding.

Today, sadly, holy wells with tremendous significance for the communities that used them have been neglected and allowed to disappear. They are filled in, knocked down, built on, erased from the landscape, and with their passing yet more evidence for our ancestors' thoughts, beliefs and feelings disappears with them.

****

Appendix 1. Ownership of Ffynnon Elian.

In 1686 William Pugh of Penrhyn in the county of Caernarfon, married Elizabeth Langton of Lowe Hall, Hindley, in Lancashire. Conveyed to them by Deed on the occasion of their marriage was the farmhouse known as Cefn-y-Ffynnon ('the ridge behind, or the back of, the well') and the surrounding land that included Ffynnon Elian. The farmhouse and land were in the township of Eirias, the parish of Llandrillo-yn-Rhos, and county of Caernarfonshire, a mile inland from the coast of North Wales. The farmhouse still stands. The buildings are of traditional Welsh design, the main house a series of spaces carefully sited sloping downward along a bed of rock to ensure that rain runs underneath and disappears into the fields below. Stone-built outbuildings, barns and stables, are nearby.

In 1770, when William and Elizabeth's descendents sold Cefn-y-Ffynnon, the estate was described as follows:

> All the messuages, etc, lying and situate in the township of Eirias, in Caernarfon, commonly called or known by the name of Ffynnon Elian, or Cefn and now or late in the tenure of Thomas Owen, the undertenant, all houses, edifices, barns, stables, orchards, pastures, fordings, woods, underwoods, lead, copper, coal and iron, quarries of stone, ways and wastes, waters, water courses, paths, passages, turbary and pasture etc, for all and all manner of cattle, heaths, furze etc.[19]

There is no record of when the house was built. Welsh hearth tax records began in 1662 and by that time the farmhouse had been in existence for some years. There is no Welsh equivalent to the Domesday Book, that lists every dwelling in England from the middle of the 11th century. The Hearth Tax recorded dwellings where there was more than one hearth and thus excluded many smaller dwellings. The records themselves, those that remain for Caernarfonshire and Denbighshire, name the people who owned such dwellings but not the names of the houses. For example,

---

[19] Deeds of Cefn y Ffynnon farm.

'William Pugh' owned three hearths in Llanelian in 1681 (indicating that the house had three fireplaces in it), but the name of that dwelling is not given. It is probably Cefn-y-Ffynnon farmhouse, but it is not certain.

Documentary evidence shows that the farm known as 'Cefn in Eirias' was owned by the Pugh family from sometime before 1661. The possibility is explored here of an older connection between the Pughs of Penrhyn and the messuage[20] known as 'Ffynnon Elian, or Cefn', going back to the early 16th century. The Pugh family were wealthy and well-connected and began their long occupation of Penrhyn, a large and important house in Creuddyn, Caernarfonshire, about five miles away from Cefn-y-Ffynnon, at the beginning of the 16th century.

Cefn-y-Ffynnon farmhouse.

After Edward I had conquered North Wales by the end of the 13th century he granted land and property to his supporters, known as the Marcher Lords. They in turn rented land to tenants for the succeeding three hundred years. One of the results of the Acts of Union in 1536 and 1543, as Henry VIII tried to create a united kingdom, was that new county boundaries were created. Four of the Marcher Lordships that had included much of the North Wales coastal area became the county of Denbighshire, others became Caernarfonshire. Part of the border between these two new counties was the small stream known variously as Nant-y-Ffynnon, Nant Meifod and Avon-y-Parkie that ran down to the sea next to Ffynnon Elian and land belonging to Cefn-y-Ffynnon. Boundaries often followed the older, parish boundaries (established by the late 13th century) and even earlier commote

---

[20] The dwelling houses, outbuildings and curtilage (gardens and orchards) and the land they are built on.

boundaries. Ffynnon Elian stands on the commote boundary between Isdulas and Uwchdulas, the parish boundary between Llandrillo-yn-Rhos and Llanelian-yn-Rhos, and on the county boundary between Caernarfonshire and Denbighshire.

New generations of land-owners began to establish themselves in their large estates, leased from Marcher Lords. The *uchelwyr* (gentry) families of Welsh origin, Mostyns, Wynnes, and Bulkeleys, began leasing and renting land, and the Pughs, forefathers of William, did so also from the beginning of the 16th century.

The Pughs of Penrhyn, as they became known, lived in Creuddyn[21] from the early 16th century, an area at the eastern end of Caernarfonshire. In the 16th century the family were wealthy and well-connected. They were the tenants and residents of the only manor house in Creuddyn mentioned by John Leland in his *Itineraries* (1538 to 1543), who noted, 'Penrine, ancient stone house'. The house either was, or appeared, old then. Penrhyn is the only manor in Creuddyn on Saxton's map of 1575. It was probably known in the 16th century as Plas Penrhyn (Penrhyn Place). The house still stands in the shadow of the Little Orme, near to Llandudno on the North Wales coast. Penrhyn Old Hall, as it is now known is much altered, its chapel in ruins, though 16th century paintings can still be seen on the walls in an upstairs room of the house.

The first known owner of Penrhyn was not a Pugh, but a descendant of the warrior Ednyfed Fychan (1170-1246). Fychan was a seneschal (steward) of the Kingdom of Gwynedd and served the Welsh prince Llywelyn the Great, and his son, Dafydd ap Llywelyn. In the early 16th century, his descendant Rheinallt ap[22] Ieuan lived at Penrhyn with his wife Elisabeth, the daughter of Sir Foulke Salesbury. She was a member of the wealthy and important Salesbury family although it is not clear exactly who her father was. A 'Sir Foulke Salesbury' was the first Protestant Dean of St Asaph cathedral church in the middle years of the 16th century. It seems unlikely that he would have been a married man but he is known to have had a daughter named Elisabeth. There are other candidates with the same name from Lleweni or Rug, both large Salesbury estates. The Salesbury/Salusbury/Salisbury family were numerous, wealthy, important and influential.[23]

---

[21] Creuddyn was a sub-district of Caernarfonshire, containing four parishes.

[22] 'ap' means 'son of' in Welsh.

[23] The Salesbury family were originally either from Austria or Lancashire.

Penrhyn Old Hall.

The chapel at Penrhyn Old Hall.

Rheinallt and Elisabeth had a son, Hugh, who was about 5 years old when his father died in 1535. On his father's death, with the reversion of the estate to the crown, Hugh automatically became a ward of King Henry Vlll, indicating the elevated status of the family. Elisabeth, widow, mother of one young royal ward, occupant of Penrhyn and young enough to have more children, was a tempting prize, and within a short time she married again. Her second husband was Robert ap Hugh of Cefn-y-Garlleg, who adopted her son, and moved into Penrhyn. The Pugh (ap Hugh) family of Penrhyn was established.

Robert ap Hugh had married very well. Cefn-y-Garlleg, five miles from Penrhyn was a sizeable and successful farm but marriage with a member of the Salesbury family and a move into Plas Penrhyn was a decidedly upwardly-mobile move. After marrying Elisabeth he became a JP, an MP and a High Sheriff in Caernarfon.

In 1544, Henry Vlll approved a grant to Robert ap Hugh of:

> …lands in Penrhyn, Iroos [Eirias] Glothayth [Gloddaeth] and Rosserry Co Caernarfon, which belonged to Reginald ap Ievan [Rheinallt ap Ieuan] and are in the King's hands by the minority of Hugh ap Reginald [Hugh ap Rheinallt] son and heir of the said Reginald [Rheinallt], with wardship and marriage of the said heir. 1st Feb Henry Vlll.

And in 1551, the transfer took place as Hugh ap Rheinallt (aged 21) was granted:

> …general livery of a place or manor and lands in Penrhyn and Yreos [Eirias] co. Caernarfon.

The granting of the 'general livery' of his inherited land in 1551 to Hugh would have taken place at his coming of age (21). By then he may even have been married. His step-father, Robert ap Hugh, arranged for Hugh to marry his, Robert ap Hugh's, sister, Katrin. It was Hugh and Katrin's first living son, Robert Pugh, born in 1560, who inherited Penrhyn and whose descendants lived at Penrhyn for generations to come. David, the eldest son of Robert ap Hugh and Elisabeth, whose date of birth is not known but who could have been much older than Young Robert, inherited Cefn-y-Garlleg. The 'lands in Yreos [Eirias]' were inherited by the Pughs of Penrhyn.

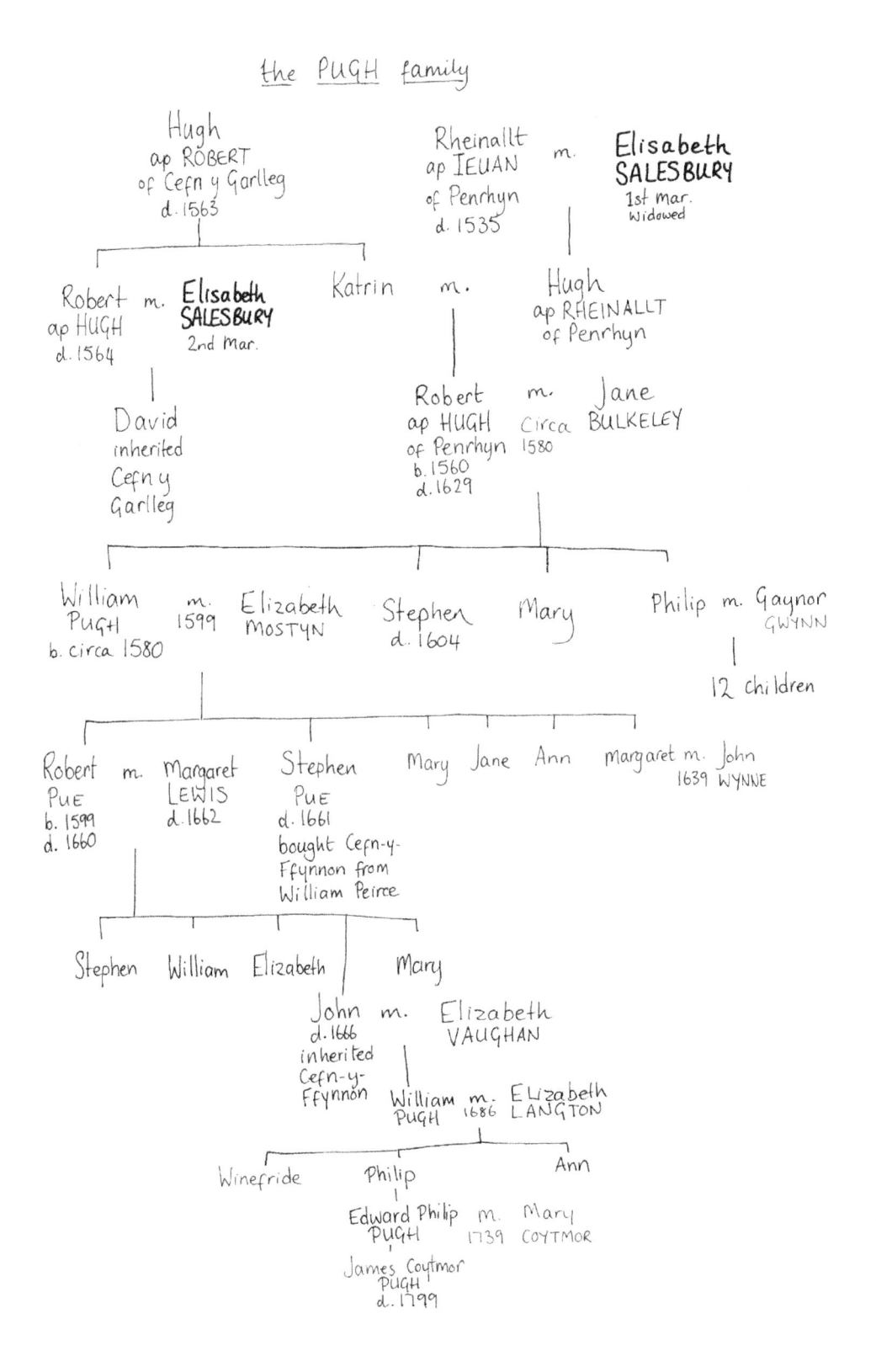

The Pugh family tree.

There is no precise record of the lands 'in Yroos' [Eirias] that were owned by Rheinallt ap Ieuan, and passed down to his son. However, a property in Eirias was named in the will of Robert ap Hugh's father, Hugh ap Robert of Cefn-y-Garlleg, who died in 1563. Hugh ap Robert bequeathed to Dafydd ap Lloyd ap Robert (possibly a grandson):

> …a tenement called Myvot in Eirias, [known today as Meifod] …which I bought of Rynalt ap John.

Meifod borders Cefn y Ffynnon lands on the south side. If 'Rynalt ap John' is in fact Rheinallt ap Ieuan,[24] then Hugh ap Robert and Rheinallt ap Ieuan were not only neighbours whose families had intermarried, but they had also bought and sold from one another the lease of land bordering Ffynnon Elian in the early decades of the 1500s. This bequest makes clear that 'Myvot' was *not* part of the lands in 'Yroos' that were passed down to Hugh ap Rheinallt when he reached his majority. The lease had been sold to Hugh ap Robert while Rheinallt was still living.

Hugh ap Robert (d.1563) lived for 25 years or so after his son Robert married Elisabeth of the Salesbury family, widow of Rheinallt ap Ieuan. He saw Elisabeth's son, Hugh, marry his, Hugh ap Robert's, own daughter, Katrin, and he was able to greet his grandson (and step great-grandson), Robert ap Hugh ap Rheinallt, who was born to Hugh and Katrin in 1560.

Young Robert, Hugh ap Robert's grandson, step great-grandson and heir to Penrhyn and surrounding land in Eirias, was, in the fashion of the wealthy families of the time made a ward of a member of one of the important, local families; Sir Richard Bulkeley of Anglesey. The wardship was the more essential because young Robert's step-grandfather and uncle, Robert ap Hugh, husband of Elisabeth and founder of the Pugh dynasty, died in 1564, only a year after his own father, Hugh ap Robert. Young Robert's parents, Hugh and Katrin, are not mentioned in Robert ap Hugh's will of 1564, and may well have died before then.

Robert ap Hugh's will of 1564 provides more information concerning the ownership of the land around Ffynnon Elian:

> I do give and bequeath to William ap Richard ap William the lease and terme of yeares that I have in the demesne of Edward Conway, so that the said

---

[24] In early documents 'Jevan' is a Welsh version of 'John' and anglicisation of 'Ieuan'.

> William ap Richard ap William do not bargaine or sell it to any other person but shalle kepe it to his life during the yeares.

Robert ap Hugh left to 'William ap Richard ap William' a lease for life on land owned by Edward Conway. There is no indication in the will of where that land was. However, in 1579, fifteen years later, the Earl of Leicester granted Edward Conway more land. Edward Conway now acquired 34 acres lying in Dynerth, a township in Llandrillo parish. This land lay 'in the Dynerth township' along 'a stream dividing the Counties of Denbigh and Caernarfon'. This 'stream', on the county boundary and known in part variously as Nant-y-Ffynnon, Nant Meifod and Avon-y Parkie, runs next to Ffynnon Elian. The Conway lands can be established as being next to, or including, those of Cefn-y-Ffynnon in 1579. There is also the strong possibility that the 'new' lands acquired by Edward Conway were adjacent to the 'older' lands, leased by Robert ap Hugh and left in perpetuity to 'William ap Richard ap William'.

The Mostyn family papers help to further establish land ownership later in the 16th century. They contain an entry recording that in 1586 a tenement was conveyed by Piers ap William ap Ithell, yeoman of Eirias, Caernarfonshire, to John Rosyndall (otherwise known as John Lloyd, mercer, of Denbigh). The tenement was Tythen-y-Parkie (known now as Parciau farm). Parciau borders Cefn-y-Ffynnon on the north side between Cefn-y-Ffynnon and the sea. The tenement was:

> …lying in length between the lands of Edward Conway Esq and the lands of Piers ap Ithell, and in breadth between the lands of the same Edward Conway and a stream called Avon y Parkie. Also a moiety of a meadow called Gwergloth y Parkie, lying in breadth between the lands of the said Piers ap Ithell and the said stream and in length between the lands of Robert Peughe and the lands of the said Piers ap Ithell: and one *lez ffrith* called Maes Gwyn lying between the lands of the said Piers ap Ithell and the said Robert Peughe.

It is clear that in 1586 the Peughes (Robert Pugh of Penrhyn) and the Conways together with Piers ap Ithell owned or leased the land surrounding Ffynnon Elian. Presumably the Conways' land was on the north side, towards the sea and the Pughs' land encompassed Cefn-y-Ffynnon and Ffynnon Elian, inland to the south. Meifod farm, owned by the Pughs of Cefn-y-Garlleg (David Pugh), lies immediately south of Ffynnon Elian, on the other side of Groes Road.

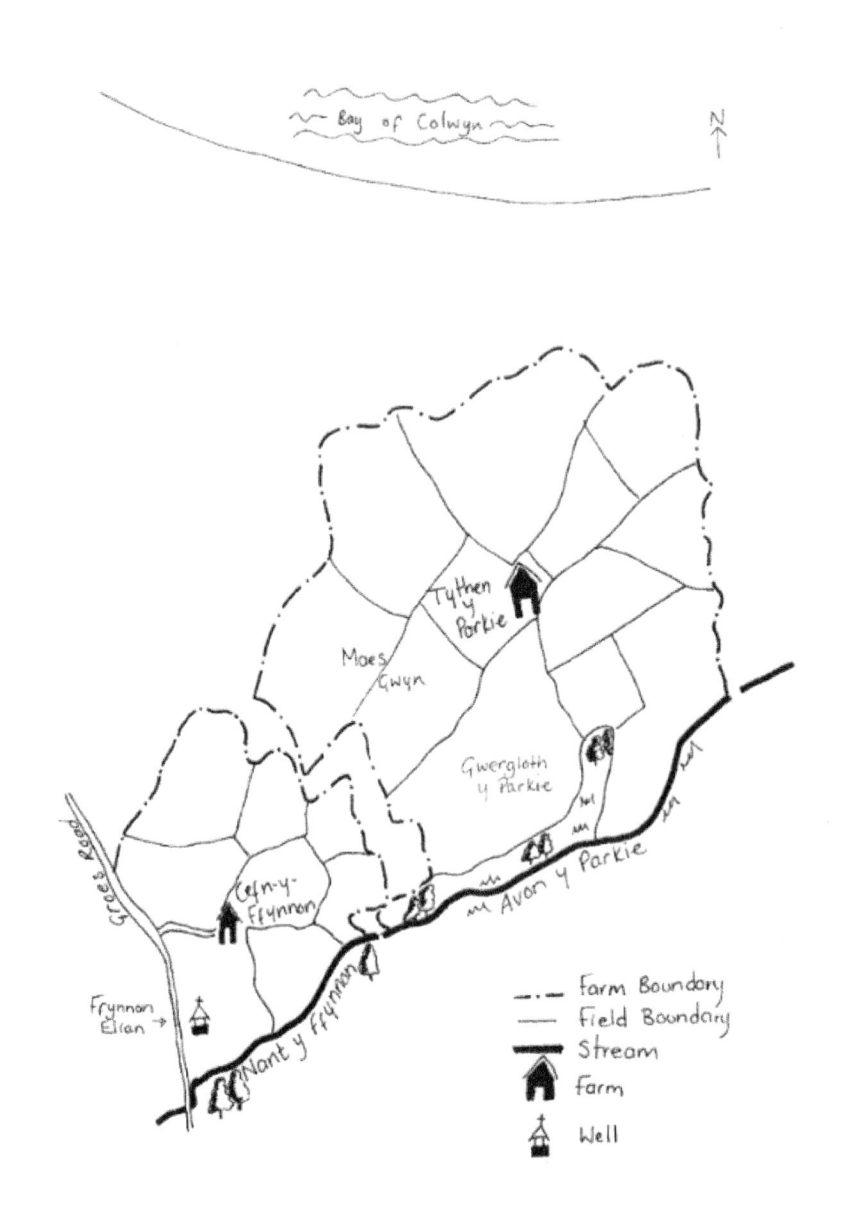

There is one more link in Robert ap Hugh's will of 1564 between the Pughs and the Cefn-y-Ffynnon land that included Ffynnon Elian. At the end of his will, Robert ap Hugh named Richard Peirce, who was left some money and described as a 'clerke'. A 'clerke' was a cleric, rather than an administrator, and in medieval Britain the word also indicated a 'scholar'. The link is as follows: in 1661, nearly one hundred years later, Stephen Pue, Robert Pugh's step great-grandson, wrote in his will:

> …I do give and bequeath all that messuage and lands called Cefn in Eirias in the Commott of Creythyn and the county of Caernarfon that I bought of William Peirce, to my nephew John for the terme of his natural life.

'Peirce' in this spelling is not a common name (derived from 'ap Rhys' it is changed to 'Prys', 'Pyers', 'Price', or the much more usual spelling 'Pierce'), although it must be stressed that erratic spelling was commonplace. In his will of 1564, Robert ap Hugh left land to 'William ap Richard ap William in the demesne of Edward Conway'. I think it is possible that the names 'Richard' and 'William' were repeated down the generations in the Peirce family, as the names Hugh and Robert were in the Pugh's, and that 'William ap Richard ap William' who inherited a permanent lease of land was possibly the son of Richard Peirce, 'Clerke' who was left money. I also think it is possible that the land bequeathed to 'William ap Richard ap William' in Robert ap Hugh's will of 1564 was the same land, 'Cefn in Eirias', that Stephen Pue bought back from William Peirce, at some time before Stephen's death in 1661. Further proof of a connection between the two families was the marriage, in 1662, between Jane, the daughter of William Pugh, and Richard Peirce.

The connection between the Pughs, the Peirce family and land around Cefn-y-Ffynnon continued. In 1675, Robert Pugh of Cefn-y-Garlleg took out a mortgage on part of the land at 'Myvot'. In 1694, Robert Pugh and his son, Hugh Pugh, together with Edward Peirce of Llysfaen (a parish bordering Llanelian-yn-Rhos), took 'lease of possession of a messuage called Tythyn Myvot [Meifod] and parcels of land, all situated in Kilgwin, Co. Denbigh'. Edward Peirce was probably the owner of 'Ty Mawr' in Llysfaen. In 1699 in *Parochialia* Edward Lhwyd put 'Ty Mawr' and its owner Edward Peirce at the top of his list of 'Tai Kryvivol' (important houses) in Llysfaen.

In his will of 1564 Robert ap Hugh gave Young Robert, his nephew and step-grandson, aged four, as ward to Sir Richard Bulkeley. Robert ap Hugh also left a legitimate son David, who must have still been under-age although somewhat older than Young Robert, as ward of Sir John Salesbury (a member of Elisabeth's immediate family). David inherited the Cefn-y-Garlleg estate. Young Robert inherited Penrhyn and all the lands in Eirias. A condition of Robert's wardship was that he married one of Sir Richard's daughters and Young Robert duly married Jane Bulkeley, probably around 1580.

In 1586 Robert Pugh, aged 26, was a listed recusant living in Penrhyn. He was married to Jane, the daughter of Sir Richard Bulkeley, as promised in the terms of the wardship set up by his step-grandfather (and uncle), Robert ap Hugh. In 1582 a 'writ of outlawry' had been issued against him, either for non-payment of recusancy fines, or a refusal to go to church for Protestant services. In 1583 Robert Pugh was listed as a '…recusant of 12 months standing' and in 1587 an anonymous writer noted that '…there were always notorious recusants at Penrhyn'. The chapel at Penrhyn, in ruins but still standing today, would have been used as often as he dared in the middle and later years of the 16th century for Mass and other Catholic services. Succeeding generations of Pughs remained Catholic and recusant.

Robert Pugh's dedicated Catholicism may have been inherited. In the preamble to his will in 1563, Hugh ap Robert, whose daughter, Katrin, was Robert's mother, bequeathed his soul into the:

> …merciful hands of Almightie God my Maker and Redeemer, trusting to be saved through the miracle of his bitter passion, desiring the blessed Virgin Marie and all the holie company of heaven to praye for me, and my bodie to be buried in Christian burial.

In 1564, a year later, Robert ap Hugh, Young Robert's step-grandfather (and uncle) asked in the preamble to his will only to '…bequeath my soule to Almighty God', the standard wording of Protestant wills at that time.

It is possible that the mention of the 'Virgin Marie and all the holie company of heaven' is an indicator of Hugh ap Robert's Catholicism. Even bearing in mind that it was relatively easy for families living a long way away from large towns to disregard the growing intolerance towards Catholics, overt mention of the 'blessed Virgin Marie' and the 'holie company of heaven' was unusual by 1563, the fifteenth year of Elizabeth's reign. Religious doctrine and worship were still the subject of intense discussion. The final version of the *Thirty Nine Articles* of faith was not accepted until 1571.

Robert ap Hugh's will in 1564 reflected his position in life. He enjoyed public office as JP, MP and High Sheriff; positions he could not have held as a listed recusant Catholic. However, the reason for questioning his essential beliefs, those of his wife

Elisabeth and of the Bulkeley and Salesbury families is that Young Robert ap Hugh ap Rheinallt (1560 – 1629), known as Robert Pugh, grew up in their care and was a listed recusant in his early 20s. And he remained one of the most passionately dedicated Catholics Wales has ever known, and died as one.

Robert and Jane visited Lancashire frequently, staying with the Langtons of Lowe Hall and the Houghtons, both recusant families (one hundred years later in 1686 his direct descendent, William Pugh, married Elizabeth Langton). Robert encouraged the training of Catholic priests in Douai, helped priests to minister to local Catholic families and he protected, supported and befriended one of the few Welsh martyrs and the only one to be put to death in Wales during the reign of Elizabeth I, the Blessed William Davies.

William Davies was born at Groes yn Eirias, sometime in the middle of the 16th century. Groes yn Eirias is a crossroads a few miles from Penrhyn, and within easy walking distance of Ffynnon Elian. He grew up as the net tightened around Catholics but as punishments became ever more severe he determined to become a priest, trained abroad, and returned to serve the Catholic families in North Wales.

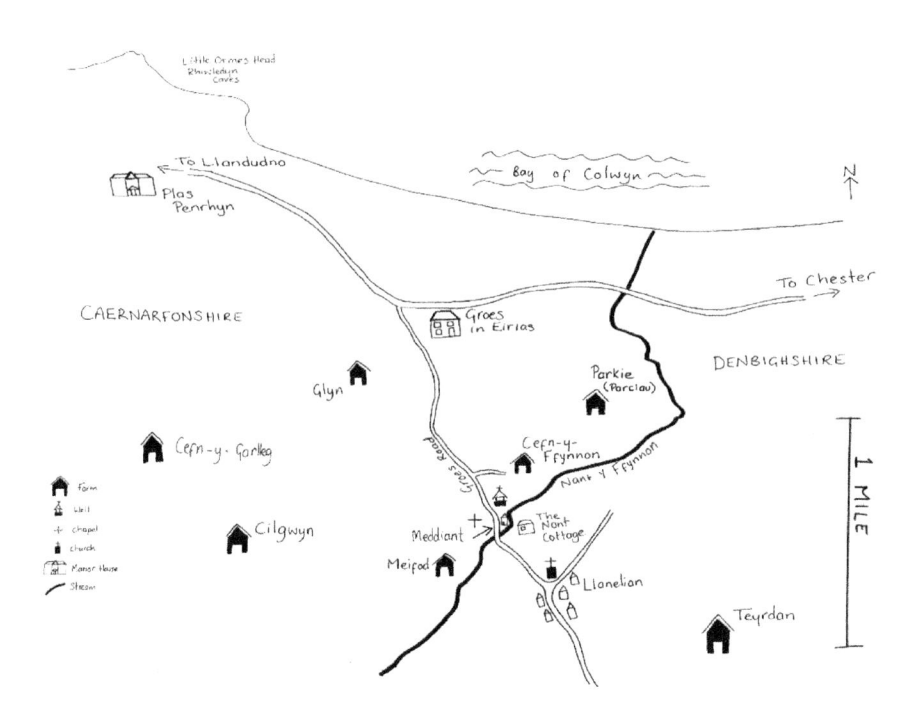

The wider area.

William Davies and Robert Pugh planned and initiated one of the most daring schemes to promote Catholicism. They decided to print and disseminate Catholic literature from the Rhiwledyn caves (known today as the Little Orme) close to Penrhyn. The reading or printing of Catholic literature was forbidden by law, with heavy penalties that became treasonable and thus punishable by death as the century wore on and Elizabeth became more and more fearful of a Catholic claim to her crown. At some time in late 1586 or early 1587 a group of men, led by Robert Pugh, constructed a printing press inside a cave at the back of the cliffs, looking out to sea. They lined the walls of the cave with wooden panels, brought in supplies, set up an altar, and went to work. The pamphlet they produced was the first printed material to be produced in Wales, a devotional work on the proper service of God. The imprint 'Rouen 1585' appeared at the front of *Y Drych Christianogawl* (the Christian Mirror) to conceal the existence of the printing press in a cave in North Wales. William Davies was present in the cave at various times, either to help with the printing work, or more probably to conduct Catholic services for the men there. He is described as *Syr William, seren ei wlad* (star of his country) by Gwylim Pue, grandson of Robert, who commemorated the events in the cave in verse.

The probable site of the cave at the back of Rhiwledyn (Little Orme).

In April 1587, the local Justice, Sir Thomas Mostyn, was roused by a suspicious neighbour of the Pughs and enjoined to investigate the caves at Rhiwledyn. Sir Thomas reported that there was no one at the cave, though the means of survival could be seen inside and pieces of lead type were found in the sand nearby. On 19 April that year, Sir William Griffith wrote to the Archbishop of Canterbury (Whitgift), expressing his outrage that the inhabitants of the cave had been allowed to evade capture. His grovelling apologies may have been genuine, or may have been for the Archbishop's benefit. The Mostyns were possibly Catholic sympathisers, and Sir Thomas had perhaps allowed the men to escape. Whatever Griffith's personal feelings, he would certainly have wanted to hold on to his job as Chancellor of Bangor, and to be seen to uphold the law. After decades of religious change and upheaval, it was not easy to know where true belief lay in the many men who accepted outward conformity but may well have remained Catholic sympathisers. Recusants nailed their colours to the mast and relied on these 'sympathisers' to help the cause in other ways. Both William Davies and Robert Pugh went into hiding after escaping from the Rhiwledyn caves. They helped to identify and encourage young Catholics who wanted to train as priests abroad, contacted and supported other recusants, and hid priests who would say mass whenever and wherever they could.

William Davies was hanged, drawn and quartered in Beaumaris in July 1593 after he was caught in Holyhead, once more with Robert Pugh, trying to arrange ship's passage for four students to the new seminary in Valladolid in Spain. Hostility to Foulk Thomas, a zealous local Protestant who had made the arrests, enabled Robert Pugh to escape. A letter to the Bishop of Bangor at the time makes clear that many named arresting officers were so reluctant to do 'their duty' that they too were arrested. Robert Pugh died in 1629 after years of escaping capture or prosecution for his Catholicism, and is buried in Llandrillo churchyard, a mile or two from Penrhyn, with many members of his family. It appears that he was able to practise his faith until he died, as he is listed for recusancy in Caernarfon in 1607.

Robert and Jane Pugh had three sons; William, Stephen and Philip (Phylip) and a daughter, Mary. Philip, a listed recusant, married Gaynor Gwyn and had twelve living children. All seven of Philip and Gaynor's sons worked to promote Catholicism and many died abroad. Their eldest son, Robert, died in Newgate

Prison for his beliefs. Gwilym, another son, is the author of the poem commemorating the Blessed William Davies in the Rhiwledyn caves. Stephen died abroad, unmarried, in 1604.

William, probably Robert's oldest son, married Elizabeth Mostyn, daughter of William Mostyn of Basingwerk, Co. Flint in 1599. A year earlier in 1598 William Pugh had been 'assessed for Penrhyn Lands'.[25] The Mostyns were (and have remained) one of most financially and socially successful families in North Wales. The marriage of a daughter to a known, listed recusant suggests strongly that they were heartfelt Catholic sympathisers, if not recusants themselves. The recusant rolls noted that a 'William Pugh of Bodlennyn, Gent and his wife Elizabeth Mostyn' were listed recusants in 1605. 'Bodlennyn' was the name of the village surrounding the church in Llanelian. It is possible that William and Elizabeth were living in Cefn-y-Ffynnon itself.

William and Elizabeth had several children. Their eldest son, Robert (1599 – 1660) married Margaret Lewis. Stephen, their second son, who died unmarried in 1661, is the first Pugh to claim specific ownership in writing of the messuages and lands of Cefn-y-Ffynnon that included Ffynnon Elian. In his will of 1661 he left the estate, 'Cefn in Eirias' that he 'bought of William Peirce', to his nephew John, son of his brother Robert. John Pue married Elizabeth Vaughan, and died young, in 1666. He was the father of William Pugh, to whom Cefn-y-Ffynnon was conveyed by Deed in 1686, on his marriage to Elizabeth Langton. Elizabeth was a member of the family that William's great-grandparents, Robert and Jane, visited in Lancashire in the last decades of the 16th century.

Generations of Pughs probably remained Catholic, although the list of recusants in Caernarfonshire is incomplete. The recusant Langtons of Lowe, however, kept a priest stationed with them at Lowe Hall. Dom Placid Acton, a Benedictine, lived there from 1699 until his death in 1729 and mass was said 'as opportunity afforded'. The long relationship between the Pughs and the Langtons, resulting in the marriage of William and Elizabeth in 1686 is evidence of enduring Catholic belief within the Pugh family and close continuing connection with Catholic recusant families in Lancashire.

---

[25] This was common practice for listed recusants. Their fines were determined by what they owned.

But by the 1770s, 200 years after William Davies and Robert Pugh fought so hard to promote and sustain Catholicism in Wales, the Pughs' fortunes had depleted. Centuries of struggle against Protestantism and being named as recusants had deprived them of well-paid and important positions in the local area and the crippling fines they had paid as recusants for so long had diminished their status and their coffers. The last of the Pughs, James Coytmor Pugh had inherited the Penrhyn and Coytmor estates as a result of his father's marriage to Mary Coytmor in around 1780. His great grandfather William Pugh's marriage to Elizabeth Langton in 1686 had helped to increase the family fortunes and had brought substantial property in Lancashire to James' father, Edward Philip Pugh, but Lowe Hall, the Langton's family home, was sold by Edward Philip Pugh to the Duke of Bridgewater for £6,500 in 1765. Numerous Pugh properties in North Wales, including Penrhyn and Cefn-y-Ffynnon, were sold before James' death in 1799.

Appendix 2. Who was Saint Elian?

Ffynnon Elian is named for Elian, a Welsh saint. Holy wells in Wales are often named for local saints, as are early Welsh churches that commemorate the presence of a saint in the local landscape. The prevalence of names beginning with 'Llan' and followed by a saint's name, especially in North Wales, bears testimony to the influence of the early saints and their proselytising work among the local population. St Elian was one of the most important saints in north west Wales, especially in Anglesey and he has left a legacy of place names. As well as two churches in his name there are two wells that have both been known as blessing and cursing wells and farms, fields and mountains are named after him. There is a third well in his name, in Betws Gwerfil Goch, 30 miles south east of Llanelian but there is no recorded history of this well. This legacy indicates a fairly influential and long-lasting *cultus*. Elian's 'first' church, Llaneilian, is near to Amlwch in North Anglesey. His later church is in Llanelian, a village on the North Wales coastline, some 43 miles away. Both churches have holy wells bearing Elian's name. In Anglesey, Ffynnon Eilian (the slightly different spelling is probably earlier than 'Elian') is still to be found in the rocks along the coastline of northern Anglesey. However, it is Ffynnon Elian that became notorious as 'the Cursing Well', and similar use at Ffynnon Eilian, only noted by Elias Owen at the end of the 19th century, may have been imitation of its more famous namesake.

What is known about St Elian comes from three documentary sources. The legend of the creation of St Elian's Well is the familiar trope of a wandering saint on pilgrimage (in this instance perhaps on the way to St Asaph from Bangor) who sat at the side of the road and pushed his staff into the ground whereupon a spring of pure water flowed up immediately. In this mythic re-creation of the origins of a holy well the saint then blessed the water and prayed that anyone who asked anything of God could henceforth ask for it at this spring, in the saint's name. The origins of this tale are not to be found in the three documents that provide all the information available on St Elian. The legend of the wandering saint is likely to be a relatively late adoption of a familiar trope.

The suggestion that St Elian himself ever came to Ffynnon Elian or nearby is impossible to prove, but not unlikely. There is the name of the well, Saint Elian's Well. A nearby field is 'cae meudwy' (the hermit's field) and the field name where the well is situated is 'cae Ffynnon Elian' (St Elian's well field). A nearby hill is named Mynedd Elian. The church is and always was, named for St Elian, and the surrounding village became known as Llanelian at the beginning of the 14th century, possibly because of increased interest in the *cultus* of Elian, his well and his church.

Probably the oldest documentary evidence for Saint Elian is *Bonedd y Saint* (The Genealogies of the Saints), a list of early Welsh saints that includes 'Elien Keimyad, m. alltu redegauc'. (Elian Ceimiad, the son of Alltu Redegog). The *Bonedd* was first put into one of many manuscript forms in the early 13th century, but is from older sources. 'Keimyad' ('ceimiad') has been translated as 'champion'.

A later documentary source for St Elian/Elien/Aelian/Eilian is a *cywydd* (poem) written by Gwilym Gwyn around 1500. In the traditional hagiography of the Welsh Saints, *cywyddau* were composed from the 11th century onwards, using material that has often disappeared although where lives of the saints have survived, the poetry reflects this. Gwyn's *cywydd* is a late and incomplete recollection and celebration of the life of Elian, but it is the only one we have. The 'history' of Elian as told in the *cywydd* is as follows.[26] Elian's sainthood began early on Anglesey as he defended his father, Alltu Redegog/redegauc. From within his mother's womb, Elian cried out to his father, who was then able to behead a surprise attacker, an Irishman. Relations between the Irish and the Welsh worsened swiftly after the Romans left Britain. When the Romans withdrew from Wales from the 5th century onwards and were no

---

[26] Ed. Barry J Lewis, *Medieval Welsh Poems to Saints and Shrines*, Dublin, 2015.

longer helping the indigenous population of Anglesey to ward off Irish attacking forces, skirmishes and battles begin to be recorded. Elian's actions in defending his parents from an Irishman may be a symbolic representation of historical truth.

Elian's father is known as a 'champion', from the story of his bravery, and Elian is called a 'saint' in his mother's womb. He is also described as being 'reckoned, pope of Rome'. He raised two people from the dead and spoke 'in most excellent sermon', but (and here the text is incomplete) he seems to have resigned the papacy and returned to his native Anglesey. Elian sailed back to his homeland, with his men, his oxen and his chattels, through a 'green topped ocean', and landed at Porth yr Ychain, in Anglesey, where even today the mark of his oxen's hooves may apparently still be seen.

The third source of information on Elian's life takes up the story from here, and helps to place Elian's lifespan in the late 5th and 6th centuries. The 'Carta Eliani'[27] is a much-redacted copy of what purports to be an agreement between Elian and Cadwallon Lawhir, king of Gwynedd from 450 – 51 AD. The charter is clearly dedicated to 'Elianus' but almost immediately the 'blessed Hyllarie' is named as the subject of the text. The names 'Elian' and 'Hilary' are used interchangeably throughout the text of the Charter, and the *cywydd* seems to strongly suggest that they were one and the same person, both bishops and later, popes. Their names are used throughout the history of St Elian's church in Llanelian-yn-Rhos although there would seem to be no connection between the two saints. St Hilary, a 4th century saint, became Bishop of Poitiers, never visited Wales, and lived at least a hundred years before Elian. The immediate explanation is found in the feast days of Elian and Hilary, both on 13 January. Saints' feast days were typically assigned by the Church if the day of the saint's death was known. If that day was 'taken' then a nearby day was assigned and as there were so many canonised saints by the early Middle Ages there was considerable overlap and many saints now share a feast day. Exactly when and in what circumstances the saint's feast day was assigned is difficult to ascertain. 'Carta Eliani', like the *Bonedd* and the *cywydd*, was written many hundreds of years after the events it describes, and the conflation between the two saints, Hilary and Elian, has continued until the early 20th century. Both names are used in 18th and 19th century Llanelian church documents although St Hilary appears more often in English documents and Welsh devotees of St Elian would not have

---

[27] Anon, 'Charta Sti. Eliani, in Anglesey', *Cambrian Journal* (1863).

heard of Hilary. The continuing use of 'Hilary' by religious commentators writing in English in the 18th and 19th centuries may have come from lingering memories of the 'Charter' and the early Welsh church calendar, or just the assumption of a straightforward translation from the Welsh name of Elian. What is clear from the continuing interchangeable use of the saints' names is the prime importance of saints' feast days over individual saintly cults until the end of the 19th century.

'Carta Eliani' recorded the story of Saint Elian's life after his return from Rome. Elian restored the sight of King Cadwallon, who in return granted to Elian a substantial amount of land in north-east Anglesey. There is confusion in the telling of the tale in the Charter and a suspicion that Elian himself caused the King's blindness after Cadwallon had stolen cattle from him. After the cattle were 'returned tenfold', Cadwallon's sight was then restored, and land granted to Elian in perpetuity. Another *cywydd* that has never been found in its original form is quoted in Henry Rowland's publication of 1723, *Mona Antiqua Restorata*. This fragment supports the theory that Cadwallon stole Elian's cattle and was struck blind by the saint in punishment before having his sight restored again:

Elian wneath i rai wylo	Elian made some weep with anger
O lid am ei fuwch a'i lo,	For his cow and calf
Fe wnaeth yn ddall Gaswallon	He struck Caswallon blind
Arglwydd mawr yngogledd Mon	The great Lord of north Anglesey.

'Carta Eliani' ends with Cadwallon asking Hyllarie if he is willing to come to 'the East', with 'armour and footmen'. This is clearly a reference to the Crusades which took place between 1095 and 1291, presumably the period when the Charter was being written. Pressing contemporary issues had rather displaced the, by then, ancient story of St Elian.

Why was a 'second' Elian settlement established 45 miles away from north Anglesey? A possible explanation can be suggested in the achievements of Elian's protector and king, Cadwallon. King Cadwallon Lawhir ruled over Anglesey, the Lleyn peninsula and much of the Snowdon area but his main residence and castle is thought to have been at Bodysgallen, just outside what is now the town of Llandudno and about five miles away from Llanelian. This was the eastern edge of his kingdom, and perhaps he chose to live close to the border to be ready for possible attack from eastern Wales and England. He is thought to have built another castle or residence near to Bodysgallen known as 'Vardre' in Deganwy on the banks of the river Conwy. Cadwallon's son, Maelgwn, king of Gwynedd after his father, is said to have lived at Vardre and to have built and dedicated a church near Deganwy at some time in the middle of the 6th century. The church was known at one time as St Hilary's. It is the oldest church in the area, the only 'Hilary' church and Maelgwn died there, legend has it, praying to be cured of yellow fever. It is possible that Maelgwn took the name directly from the Charter drawn up between his father and Elian and that Elian's followers and even Elian himself may have come to this easternmost edge of Cadwallon and Maelgwn's kingdom to set up a religious house to minister to the king and increase the king's status in the area. In the absence of any written evidence of any kind, it is only possible to speculate as to why another Elian church sprang up so far away from the original Eilian church in north Anglesey. Llanelian in Denbighshire at the furthest reaches of the kingdom of Cadwallon, and his son, Maelgwyn is 45 miles away from St Eilian's church in Anglesey.

Could St Elian or his followers have settled in the very early middle ages in Llanelian-yn-Rhos? An indication of religious settlement during the last half of the first millenium was the establishment of a *clas* church or monastic grouping, where monks gathered to live and work together in small groups under the leadership of an *Abad* (Abbot). Llanelian church is not on the list of verified *clas* churches but has a discernible, circular, boundary. This is by no means evidence of an Elian monastery, but an indication, with the Elian names in the nearby area, of early habitation.

Another indication of the establishment of a monastic grouping on the site of the present church is in the name of the village before it became known as Llanelian-yn-Rhos in the early 14th century. Church Tax records show that the older name was 'Bodlennin' (with variant spellings 'Bodwelennin' or 'Bodlenyn'). It has not been possible to discover a meaning for the last syllables of any of these various spellings, or to trace a name from them, but 'bod' firmly indicates a dwelling place of some kind. There is a slight consonance between 'welennin', 'lenyn', 'lennin' and 'Elian' and in *Bonedd y Saint*, the spelling is 'Elien' which comes closer to the early names of the settlement. 'Bodlenyn' could possibly even be an early spelling of 'Bodleian' (the dwelling place of a nun). The connection is not strong enough to state with any certainty that 'Elian' is part of the name of the settlement before the early years of the 14th century, although it was always the name of the church. An added complication was the existence of a separate Medieval settlement between Betws-yn-

Rhos and Llanelian-yn-Rhos named 'Bodlyman' (now Rhyd-y-Foel). Another nearby settlement is Bodelwyddan. What is known is that by 1310, before the parish boundary separated the Elian well and the Elian church administratively, the village nearest to Ffynnon Elian was re-named Llanelian (and also continued to be called Bodlenyn). There would seem to be no reason for this change other than the growing importance of the saint's name, to be found at the holy well and the church.

Appendix 3. Holy Wells in Wales and the Reformation.

There is no agreed definition of a holy well. 'Holy' suggests that the well is named for a saint, yet wells with saint's names are not all of long standing, do not all have accreted legends and stories associated with them and wells with secular names have also been highly revered and valued. Water sources have always been of primary importance wherever there is a settled population, however small, and most of the wells and springs that served early human settlement have no particular name and have had no function other than supplying water. Broadly, holy wells are water sources that have greater significance for the local population, and have been used for both religious and secular purposes. The most famous of these in Wales, St Winefride's well in Holywell, Flintshire, has attracted millions of visitors over 13 centuries, and indeed continues to do so. People come to St Winefride's in search of healing (there is a room full of discarded crutches), religious worship, and to see and venerate the holy relics that have been lodged there over the centuries including a tiny fragment of St Winefride's bone. The bathing pool is where miracles of healing are reported to have taken place.

The Holy Wells of Wales by Francis Jones was published in 1954. It has been the standard work on holy wells in Wales, but his research was patchy and his references sometimes inaccurate. The work of Cymdeithas Ffynhonnau Cymru (Welsh Wells Society) has provided information on many of the less well-known wells, and Eirlys and Ken Gruffydd have published two books. Janet Bord is researching in depth the 800 plus saints' wells in Wales. In 2008 a collection of photographs of holy wells in Wales was published by Phil Cope.

Wells were a regular element of saints' cults from the earliest years of Christianity in Britain and on the continent. These shrines (or holy wells), all with a body of water as part of the worship ritual, were openly used in quite different ways throughout

Britain until the middle of the 16th century and the changes to religious observance brought about by the Protestant Reformation. These changes were radical and far-reaching and their effect on Wales and the Welsh was no less dramatic than on those living close to London, Henry VIII's seat of power. But it must also be said that these changes were implemented at different speeds, at different times and with different effects. Distance from large urban centres did allow for change to be circumvented and sometimes avoided. However, for two of the important shrines in Wales, both with a holy well, Pen Rhys in South Wales and Derfel Gadarn in the North, the Reformation spelled the end of their significance and importance as pilgrimage destinations. Their associated statues and symbols were taken down and burned in London, although the wells themselves remain.

Without contemporary written evidence, it is not possible to say with any certainty that Ffynnon Elian was active before or after the Protestant Reformation. In Wales, as elsewhere, the *uchelwyr* (gentry) would have found it expedient to appear to convert to Protestantism publicly and speedily. They had fortunes, positions and status to protect and they also had connections in and visits to London, where they would have been able to judge for themselves whether Henry VIII was likely to halt or reverse his programme of reform. After his death, and the subsequent continuing religious upheaval, those who did not identify themselves as recusants could carefully align themselves with the prevailing powers, as did many families during the second half of the 16th century and afterwards. Many people in North Wales, as elsewhere, were very careful indeed not to declare their true religious allegiances, or to ever refer to them in writing.

The Pugh family were uncompromising in their Catholicism and by the end of the 17th century they were one of the few remaining prominent recusant families in North Wales. From some time before 1661 definitely and possibly for a long time before that, they owned Ffynnon Elian and the land around it. We have Edward Lhwyd's word in *Parochialia* that Ffynnon Elian was visited by 'papists' in the 1690s, something not noted in connection with other wells and this suggests a practice of relatively long-standing. In the opinion of the writer it is highly improbable that Ffynnon Elian began to be visited by 'papists' *after* the Reformation. Much more likely is that Ffynnon Elian, with its complexity of perceived powers, was at the centre of a local cult promoted and protected by the Pugh family for centuries. With the sale of Cefn-y-Ffynnon in 1770, and the publication of Pennant's book in 1778, the reputation of Ffynnon Elian changed. 'the Cursing Well' was born, and Ffynnon

Elian became permanently known as somewhere that evil deeds born of vengeance were predominant.

Appendix 4. Cursing ritual.

When the Romans came to Britain, they brought well-defined ritual practices at specific water sources with them. They wrote their requests on lead or slate tablets, to be passed to the 'other side' through the medium of water. These tablets, known as *defixiones,* were used most often to ask for the righting of wrongs and the restoration of stolen goods, and they have been found in large numbers, not only in Bath, but also in other places associated with Roman temples, military bases or other settlement areas including Marlborough Downs, Wanborough, Hamble, Leintwardine, Chesterton, Caerleon, Pagans Hill, Brean Down and Lydney.

These tablets have been studied in connection with the places where they have been found, in an attempt to find regional variations across Britain and the continent for their use. Geoffrey Adams[28] has noted that the tablets found in the Roman settlements in Britain were used differently to those in mainland Europe. In Roman Britain, *defixiones,* or 'curse tablets' as they have often been called, were used, he says, as 'prayers for justice'. They were used when an individual felt that a wrong had been done to them and he or she then sought retribution or compensation. Adams also notes that the names on the tablets reveal that many users were not Romans, but native Britons who had adopted the use of tablets at holy wells and other water sources. These 'native' users, like the occupying Romans, were much concerned with recovering stolen goods and identifying a thief.

The use of tablets carved with the individual's name or initials by a petitioner seeking healing, justice or revenge for a perceived wrong, was recorded as being in use at Ffynnon Elian in the early 19th century, and could have been part of earlier ritual. Stones or slates with initials carved on them suggest a possible and intriguing very early connection between ritual at this well and what was British-Roman ritual practice, although *defixiones* were larger tablets of slate that contained a short message. At many wells pins, corks, bread, rags, flowers and other offerings of all kinds were recorded during the heyday of well use. Evidence of the use of personalised tablets of slate or stone has only been associated with Ffynnon Elian

---

[28] G. Adams, 'The social and cultural implications of Curse Tablets (*defixiones*) in Britain and on the continent', *Studia Humaniora Tartuensia*, 2006.

and Ffynnon Eilian, Elian's mother church in Anglesey, and only at Ffynnon Eilian in the late 19th century.

Roman presence in North Wales is now a lively area of study and discovery. A large Roman settlement has been recently uncovered on Anglesey. There were military stations in Chester and Caernarfon and roads ran along the North Wales coastline as well as inland, as the Roman army made its way towards Anglesey. A Roman road ran past the top of the village of Llanelian, very near to Ffynnon Elian. It seems unlikely but not impossible that the ritual practice at Ffynnon Elian is a surviving adaptation of ancient Roman well use.

Printed in Great Britain
by Amazon